Out of Egypt

'Offers hope and help. Healing for lesbians is reality. It does
not come overnight, nor is there some simplistic way of finding it
... the book covers a lot of ground.' – *Christianity*

'Honest and sensitive ... a practical handbook for in-depth
counselling and support.' – *Redemption*

'A practical, sympathetic and non-hysterical view. About time!'
– *Woman Alive*

Out of Egypt

*One woman's journey
out of lesbianism*

Jeanette Howard

MONARCH
BOOKS

Mill Hill, London & Grand Rapids, Michigan

First published in the UK in 1991.
Reprinted 1992, 1993, 1997. Reissued 2000.

Published in the USA by Monarch Books 2001.

Distributed by:
UK: STL, PO Box 300, Kingstown Broadway, Carlisle,
Cumbria CA3 0QS.
USA: Kregel Publications, PO Box 2607
Grand Rapids, Michigan 49501.

ISBN 1 85424 486 8 (UK)
ISBN 0 8254 6001 8 (USA)

Unless otherwise indicated, biblical quotations are from the New International Version copyright © 1973, 1978, 1984, by The International Bible Society.

British Library Cataloguing Data
A catalogue record for this book is available from the British Library.

Designed and produced for the publishers by
Gazelle Creative Productions Ltd, Concorde House,
Grenville Place, Mill Hill, London NW7 3SA.

This book is dedicated to the members of Battle Baptist Church, Battle, East Sussex. Their love for, and commitment to me, were instrumental in my walking away from lesbianism. To all of them, I offer a heartfelt 'Thank you'.

CONTENTS

Moving Towards the Land of Promise

FOREWORD

Knowing the truth and being able to work it out are often two distinct realities, especially in regard to human sexuality. Deep and baffling desires tempt us to act or fantasise in ways that we know are contrary to God's best for us. Still this knowledge of the truth may not translate into our depths. Frustration and hopelessness result.

Jeanette's book bridges that gap. She affords the lesbian struggler real hope as she walks with her along the path towards freedom. Jeanette does so by describing the interplay between God's transforming, all sufficient love and our yieldedness to it. Employing clear illustrations from the lives of lesbian strugglers, Jeanette invites us all to partake of Jesus' deep care in those areas where we dare to welcome him as a lover and restorer of the soul.

Out of Egypt rings true because Jeanette is herself a 'living epistle'. Her life proclaims Jesus' faithfulness to redeem the most persistent and confusing aspects of our personhood.

As Jeanette describes the lives of several women emerging out of lesbianism and into wholeness, we also learn of her own transformation. This authenticates her hope and yet does not impede the remarkable objectivity she displays in helping us to understand and effectively care for other women.

Jeanette extends the graspable hand of Jesus to the lesbian struggler. I am especially grateful for her book because the masculine viewpoint tends to prevail in ex-gay circles. That makes it difficult at best for the lesbian struggler to open her heart to deeper healing. She may fear that domination from men will result once she forsakes enmeshment with women. Jeanette conveys well how Jesus heals women from both expressions of brokenness. As the book unfolds, so does the truth of Jesus' faithful and very real commitment to restoring the feminine soul.

Andy Comiskey

ACKNOWLEDGEMENTS

A special thank you to Brad Sargent whose enthusiasm for, and dedication to the project, enabled me to progress past the title page. Without his support, both on a ministerial and personal level, this book would still be an idea rattling around in my head.

The following people gave freely of their time and energy to read and re-read my manuscript. Thank you for your helpful hints and suggestions.

Starla Allen	John Paulk
Darlene Bogle	Janine Puls
Al Bonnett	Gaye Rickaby
Arla Bonnett	Mona Riley
JoAnn Brandon	Debbielynne Simmons
Penny Dalton	Sandra Spencer
Bob Davies	Jody Spinuzza
Dawn Killion	Anita Worthen
Jeff Konrad	Frank Worthen
Kevin Oshiro	Arthur Worthington

Thank you to those ministries and individuals whose faithful prayers covered the work.

I also thank Love in Action International and Exodus International for their financial support while the book was being written.

AUTHOR'S NOTE

To make application of Scriptures more immediate to women, I have changed such words as *man*, *brother* and *son* to *woman*, *sister*, and *daughter*. These changes are denoted by square brackets.

Where necessary names have been changed to protect the identity of the people concerned.

Jehovah, Our Deliverer

CHAPTER ONE

EGYPT

I laid back on my bed and sighed deeply. My bedroom was so cold I could see my breath spiralling up to the ceiling. It was two-thirty in the morning and outside the usually busy road was silent. I stared at the ceiling, contemplating part of a scripture I had just read: 'You did not choose me, but I chose you to go and bear fruit—fruit that will last' (Jn 15:16).

A realisation struck me suddenly. I did not have to choose God. He had already chosen me. All I had to do was receive everything that he had to give me.

The past three months flashed through my mind. I recalled the first time a fellow teacher told me about God and his love for me. I remembered her surprised and pleased reaction when I first walked into church. I thought back to my recent Christmas vacation with another woman, my current lover. I considered her love for God, and her love for me. I experienced the sense of loss as I recalled leaving her at Sydney airport. I thought I had left God in Australia too.

But he had other ideas. As soon as I landed in England he made it clear that I had changed. Although I tried to resume my lesbian lifestyle, it felt uncomfortable and I felt out of place in it. What was once so appealing to me was now hollow. I had been around Christians for too long. Their rich quality of life and love for Jesus stood in sharp contrast to the emptiness I was now feeling.

And now he was bringing me to a point of decision. God had already primed me concerning the 'cost' of this gift of salvation. For the past month I sensed that he had been speaking to me about my lesbianism. 'I know that you believe this is all you have. But I have something better. I have the best for you.'

God never told me what the best was. But I did know that in receiving him I had to turn my back on lesbianism. I was frightened. *Won't I actually be rejecting myself and my friends? How can I explain this? Will my lesbian friends think I'm a traitor?* To give up my lesbian identity seemed impossible. Yet, in that cold winter of 1985, I knew this was the only decision I could make.

'God,' I whispered, half hoping that he wouldn't hear me, 'I don't want to play games with you. If I make this commitment and give myself to you one hundred per cent, I need you to keep your half of the bargain. I need you to be there for me.' I paused, then took the step of faith. 'Okay, God, I'm yours.'

Unexpectedly, at that moment I experienced a searing pain. My heart felt as though it had been ripped from my body. I lay there, unable to move. Then I sensed a hand resting on my chest. Slowly the piercing pain transformed into a comforting warmth.

I opened my eyes and looked around the room. *Will everything be different now?* Should I have been blinded by a dazzling light? Or heard the Hallelujah Chorus? Or seen the angels partying in heaven, celebrating my repentance? I don't know. All I know is that tears welled up in my eyes and trickled down my temples, soaking my pillow.

One question continually repeated itself in my mind: *What do I do now?* I really did not have a clue.

By turning myself over to God, I had turned my back on all that I had known from my childhood—my identity, my emotions, and my sense of purpose. Until now, my understanding of self, career, and friends had hinged on the pivotal fact that I was gay.

Now I had relinquished lesbianism—surrendered all that I had known—to follow God. I could not see him or touch him. I barely knew anything about him. *Am I out of my mind?* It seemed so crazy, but I knew it was right. But then, if it was so right, why did I feel as though I was walking out of a brightly lit place into a long, dark tunnel?

A new creation

In 2 Corinthians 5:17 God tells us: 'When someone becomes a Christian he becomes a brand new person inside. He is not the same any more. A new life has begun!' (TLB).

I was a new creation. Although I seemed to be entering a dark tunnel, in reality I was entering into my new state as a child of God. The bright light was the familiarity of sin and a lifestyle I had embraced. The darkness ahead was unknown territory.

The beginning

So many questions and fears plagued me at first. *Can I live without sex? How will I cope with loneliness? Can I have female friends and not fall into sin? How can I relate to 'real' women? Does this rejecting of my lesbianism mean that I have to marry? Can I trust God to meet all of my needs?*

I wanted to be obedient. But how was I to deal with my emotions and all those nagging questions in the forefront of my mind?

God blotted out my questions for a while. In the following days and weeks, I really sensed him carrying me through the painful 'loss' of my old life. There were times when I even forgot the pain, I was so overcome with the joy of the Lord and just being happy that I belonged to him. At other times, however, the reality of my situation would hit me. The magnitude of the task ahead seemed overwhelming, and I would question my ability to walk with God.

Giving up sex was not too hard. Ten thousand miles between you and your loved one dictates certain behavioural boundaries! But I phoned Australia at least twice a week, and wrote a letter every day. I did not launch into healthy same-sex friendships either. In actuality, I became a social recluse, venturing out only to go to church and Bible study. I was fearful of getting close to anyone because I just did not trust my wayward emotions. Although this method of Christianity did not measure up with what I had seen in Australia, I felt unable to risk going any further into the heterosexual arena.

Before long it occurred to me that I wasn't really trusting that God had my best at heart. Loneliness consumed me. Some days I accused him of just wanting to spoil my fun. Other days I sank into pity parties, claiming God had given me a rough deal and that I could not possibly be expected to uphold my part of the bargain—trusting and obeying. After all, I was only human! Other times I 'white knuckled' my way through the day, hanging on to God and forcing myself to obey when I did not really feel like it. I was determined in my will to follow God, yet my emotions were desperate to feel the love and touch of a woman.

I was finding it no simple task to leave lesbianism behind. There were no easy methods or quick fixes, devoid of any pain or discomfort, which ensured a lifelong devotion to God. Quite the contrary, I found that healing

involves facing our hurts head-on and walking through
them.

Gaining God's perspective

In order for me to remain obedient to God, I realised early
in my journey that I needed to get a correct perspective on
homosexual activity as sin. Because lesbianism felt so natural to me, I had a hard time acknowledging it for what it
is. For too long I had fallen in line with the world's view:
'If it feels good, do it.' Initially I had only the deep sense
within my conscience that lesbianism was sin. Later, as I
continued reading the Bible as a new Christian, I found
Scripture confirmed what I had already known and
accepted.

> Therefore God gave them up in the lusts of their hearts to
> impurity, to the dishonouring of their bodies among them-
> selves, because they exchanged the truth about God for a lie
> and worshipped and served the creature rather than the Crea-
> tor, who is blessed for ever! Amen. For this reason God gave
> them up to dishonourable passions. *Their women exchanged
> natural relations for unnatural*, and the men likewise gave up
> natural relations with women and were consumed with pas-
> sion for one another, men committing shameless acts with
> men and receiving in their own persons the due penalty for
> their error (Rom 1:24–27, RSV, italics mine).

Even though lesbianism had seemed natural to me, it
was not in God's sense of the natural. I had to combat my
own old, natural beliefs with God's truth on the matter.

So, in prayer, I accepted God's view on lesbianism as
being contrary to his will for my life. I agreed with God
that it was sin and assented to see lesbianism as he saw it. I
also asked God for his perspective on this issue. I needed to
sense how it grieved him when I held sin in such high
esteem.

I would love to say that this process of acting in accordance with a biblical view of lesbianism was trouble-free and immediately successful. But in truth, my flesh—my 'pull' toward the old lifestyle and its lesbian cravings—was strong. And some days, especially in the beginning, I was very unwilling to acknowledge my struggles. Although I was not acting out sexually, my fantasy life ran rampant. I rationalised with God, 'It's not as though I'm doing anything, it's only in my head!'

But God upheld his part of our bargain—being there for me *and* being in charge of my life. *He* had no intention of playing games with me.

So, obediently, I took a stand with God against my thought life too. I no longer passively accepted all the thoughts that flooded my mind, but began to measure each thought against God's standard as revealed to me in the Bible, through the Holy Spirit, and by other, more mature Christians.

There is hope

God did not forget to make provision for lesbianism. Individuals or societies may view homosexuality with disgust, but God loves us and offers a way for us to find acceptance with him, and change.

> Do you not know that the unrighteous will not inherit God's kingdom? Be no misled; neither... adulterers, nor partakers in homosexuality... will inherit the kingdom of God. And some of you were just that; but you were washed and you were made holy and you were made righteous by the power of the Lord Jesus Christ and by the Spirit of our God (1 Cor 6:9–11, Modern Language Bible).

Have you just become a Christian and know that God wants to deal with your lesbian past? Have you been a Christian most of your life, yet still struggle with homosexual temptations and relationships? Do you feel the gay lifestyle caved in on you and you finally want to finish with it? Have you already given up sex with women because you knew God said it was wrong—even though you enjoyed it—and now want to address deeper issues that inclined you towards homosexuality? Do you find yourself depending on another woman emotionally? Did you try before to leave the lesbian lifestyle, but felt disappointed by God, yourself and the church? Are you in a church leadership role, and fear others may find out your 'secret'? There is hope for change, regardless of your current situation and feelings.

Since leaving the homosexual lifestyle six years ago when I received Jesus Christ as my Lord and Saviour, I have seen God's faithfulness. Indeed, I stand in awe at what he has done in my life. Where I saw hopelessness, he saw hopefulness. Where I saw pain, he saw potential. Where I saw a disaster, he saw a daughter.

Always remember that you are not alone in your journey. I, and many other women, have left the bondage of 'Egypt' (lesbianism) and are walking into 'Canaan' (the promised land of wholeness and completeness in Christ). If you struggle with lesbianism, if your Christian road appears more like a dark tunnel than a well-lit path, if you feel overwhelmed with what is ahead of you, if you want to follow God but find your route blocked, then read on!

God delivers

I desire to share with you what I have learned of the hope and the healing that God offers us. In the coming chapters, we will consider important topics together. Some of these are:

- exploring the roots of lesbianism
- understanding attitudes and emotions
- combating loneliness

- cutting yourself free from emotionally dependent relationships
- maintaining sexual purity
- contrasting our true identity with the lesbian identity
- discovering true femininity
- experiencing real intimacy
- learning obedience
- controlling your thought life

Role models of change are of great value, so I will continue to share with you from my own experiences of growth and failings, as well as draw in the stories of other ex-lesbians. I will also refer regularly to the exodus of Israel out of Egypt, because it provides so many parallels to the healing process we go through.

This is a book about choices. God made the first choice. He chose you and me to be his precious daughters. The choice we have to make is whether or not we walk with him through the desert into the promised land.

You are about to embark on a most important journey—an exodus adventure of your own—with the God of hope leading you along the way. I know that he will be with you and bless you as you follow him out of 'Egypt' and leave lesbianism behind.

'May the God of hope fill you with all joy and peace as you trust in him, so that you may overflow with hope by the power of the Holy Spirit' (Rom 15:13).

For your information

At the back of *Out of Egypt* is a glossary. It contains definitions of counselling terms, plus 'Christianese' and other terms commonly used in discussing the Christian life, but often not defined.

For further study

For an overview of the exodus of the Israelites from Egypt to the Promised Land, you might enjoy watching the classic film, *The Ten Commandments*, starring Charlton Heston as Moses!

1. *The Cost of Commitment* by John White (Inter-Varsity Press: UK, 1976).
2. *My Utmost For His Highest* by Oswald Chambers (Barbour: USA, 1963) (UK edition: Marshalls, 1986).

CHAPTER TWO

WHO IS GOD?

Does God really love me?

One day, nearly two years after giving God charge of my life, I realised I had a great problem in my relationship with him. Although I loved God passionately, I did not really believe that he loved or could ever love me. This devotion was, in my mind, a one-way street—from me to him. Why?

In my estimation I was still too flawed to be acceptable to him. After all, I was depending on my ex-lover to fill my emotional needs. Although I didn't want to admit it, I was also looking for that perfect woman to bring me to a sense of completion. I still fantasised about old lesbian relationships and the prospect of new ones. *God doesn't love me*, I thought. *I don't even love myself.*

I devoured every Christian book I could lay my hands on, hoping to know more of God. But I became increasingly dissatisfied in my relationship with Him. Although my *knowledge* about God was increasing, I was far from *knowing* God.

My prayer times with the Lord had become dry. Without grasping the power of his love, I was left walking alone with only the use of my own resources. The strain was beginning to tell.

Questions began to consume me. *Can I continue like this for the next forty years? Is this commitment worth the loneliness I feel?* I came to a conclusion: *The only difference in my life now is that I no longer have sex.*

Although I didn't *really* believe that to be the only change in my life, somewhere along the line I was missing out on the abundant life promised me in the Bible. I had not really grasped who God was and how to plug into his resource of love.

A right perspective of God

Acknowledging my wrong belief that God did not love me was the first step. But how could I grasp hold of what God had promised in his word?

I was a member of a small Baptist church. Early on in my Christian walk, the congregation discerned a call on my life to pursue full-time Christian ministry. The only problem was that none of us knew exactly what that call entailed! So they sent me to a small Bible school in North Wales for a three-month discipleship course.

Not long after I arrived, a teacher exhorted the class to ask God for a deeper walk with him. I knew that in order to obtain that deeper walk, I had to receive his love. The first thing I did was modify Paul's prayer for the Ephesians, recorded in Ephesians 3:14–19, and make it a prayer for myself.

For this reason I kneel before you, Father. From you, your whole family in heaven and on earth derives its name. I pray that out of your glorious riches you may strengthen me with power through your Spirit in my inner being, so that Christ may dwell in my heart through faith.

And I pray that I, being rooted and established in your love, may have power, together with all the saints, to grasp

how wide and long and high and deep is the love of Christ,
and to know this love that surpasses knowledge—that I may
be filled to the measure of all your fullness, God.

I faithfully prayed that same prayer for days. Then one
night, I found myself lying face down on my bed, weeping before the Lord. I was overwhelmed with his feelings
for me. *Thank you, Daddy! You've answered my prayer*. At
long last, I *received* his love.

That was not a 'once for a lifetime' blessing, but merely
the beginning of opening up to God. As I enter new stages
of my healing process, I find the need for greater acceptance of God's love.

There is always another window to my heart that I must
open to him. This process requires vulnerability. It means
recognising my need, and allowing God to touch that
tender area.

For many of us, that is a frightening prospect. Questions regarding God's gentleness, faithfulness and trust
often arise at this time. But we must agree with who God
says he is in his Word, emotionally receive who he says he
is, and then we are able to confront those fears.

It doesn't matter how long any of us have been Christians. Unless our perspective of God is correct, we will
merely be 'marking time' instead of striding forward along
the path he has ordained for us.

As I read through the account of the Hebrew's exodus
from Egypt, I soon found out that they, too, had to gain a
new understanding of God.

God longed to reveal himself to Israel

While in Egypt, the Israelites certainly had ideas of God's
character, passed down from generation to generation for
over four hundred years. They had a knowledge about

God and some devotion to him, but they only knew God as *Elohim*—God of power and sovereignty.

The exodus began God's revelation to Israel as *Jehovah*—a personal and loving being. It was as Jehovah that God communicated so intimately with Moses, as we read in Exodus 33:11: 'The Lord [Jehovah] would speak to Moses face to face, as a man speaks with his friend.'

God continued to reveal His characteristics to Moses as Jehovah in Exodus 34:6–7: 'Then the LORD passed by in front of him and proclaimed, "The LORD, the LORD God, compassionate and gracious, slow to anger, and abounding in lovingkindness and truth; who keeps lovingkindness for thousands, who forgives iniquity, transgression and sin. . ." ' (NASB).

This new knowledge of God as Jehovah enabled the Israelites to place their trust in him. And it is into his hands as Jehovah—the personal God—that we must place ourselves.

God is fair

As stated earlier, the only way I could gain a correct perspective of God was to be in agreement, both cognitively and emotionally, with what He revealed about himself in the Bible. For instance, in my early days as a Christian, I would often find myself muttering about God's unfairness. 'If only I had a "normal" problem, life would be so much easier!'

But it is not a question of God being fair or unfair. Isaiah 59:2–3 makes it clear that it is my sin alone that keeps me separated from him: 'But your iniquities have separated you from your God; your sins have hidden his face from you, so that he will not hear. . . Your lips have spoken lies, and your tongue mutters wicked things.'

Yes, there is unfairness in the world. It is a result of the broken, sinful state of man and creation. But the reality is that God is not unfair. 1 Corinthians 1:9 states: 'God is faithful—reliable, trustworthy and [therefore] ever true to His promise, and He can be depended on; by Him you were called into companionship *and* participation with His Son, Jesus Christ, our Lord' (AMPLIFIED).

It was necessary for me to combat any misbeliefs I held with the truth of the word.

Will God abandon me?

Carol and I co-lead a weekly discipleship meeting in the San Francisco area of California. One night, after everybody had left, we chatted over a cup of coffee. We discussed various obstacles which Carol faced early in her healing process. One issue she had struggled with was fear of abandonment.

'I always clung to my lovers like a leech. When they left the apartment, if only to run an errand, I would be incredibly afraid. *What happens if she meets someone else who is more interesting than I am? Can I live without her? How will I survive on my own?*'

Of course, Carol's clinging always backfired. She smothered her lovers until they dumped her. Unfortunately, she had the same fear with God. Thoughts like these bothered her: *'If I fully give myself over to him, will he just take advantage of my emotions and then leave me all alone?'*

Carol continued, 'During the first couple of years as a Christian, I didn't really realise that I was testing God's faithfulness. My walk with him lacked closeness. Otherwise I'd have realised that I was transferring my distrust for him onto everybody else in my life.'

'Give me an example,' I probed, suspecting that I had done the same thing.

'I remember being asked by one leader of the church singles group if I wanted to go on a hike with her. Immediately I questioned her motives. *What does she want from me? What does she expect?* I agreed to go, but felt uncomfortable all afternoon.'

'Did she ask you again?'

'Oh, yes. Sometimes it was with a group of people; at other times it was just the two of us. I enjoyed her company and I wanted her friendship. But her job was mobile, and I was afraid she would be transferred to another part of the country. I determined that it was senseless to invest in someone who could leave at any given point.'

Carol stopped for a moment and shook her head in disbelief. 'It's amazing how she stuck with me, considering how I acted.'

This confused me. 'What do you mean?' I asked.

'I would say the most ridiculous things just to see how she'd react. I would accuse her of using my friendship, I would get angry, slam doors, and generally be obnoxious, just to see what she'd do. I treated other people in the same way, especially those who meant something to me.'

I looked at Carol. 'Do you know why you did this?' I asked incredulously.

'I pushed all my friends to the limit to see how far they would go to stick with me. I wanted to know the extent of their commitment. At what point would they abandon me and so give credence to my fear?'

I certainly knew from working with Carol that she didn't fear abandonment now. 'Carol,' I asked, 'what happened? What brought about such a radical change?'

Overcoming the fear of abandonment

'Well,' Carol answered, 'it was a combination of events. I acknowledged my fear. Then, through prayer, I invited the Holy Spirit to reveal the reasons why I had this problem.

'He brought to mind an incident that happened when I was three years old. My mother was hospitalised. This memory wasn't new to me, but my little-girl reaction to the event was. The Holy Spirit showed me how I had wandered around the house, confused and fearful, feeling abandoned.

'For the first time ever, I got in touch with my emotions and felt able to cry about the pain I felt at Mum's absence. There was such a release in my spirit, a real feeling of relief. And as I cried, I sensed Jesus standing next to me. He was holding my hand.'

'What happened then?' I asked.

'That was the beginning of many similar prayer sessions,' Carol said. 'In the early stages, I still feared God would abandon me. However, the greater risk I took in allowing God into those tender areas, such as the hospital incident, the more faithful he proved to be. As our relationship grew more intimate, the fear of abandonment gradually disappeared. Confidence replaced fear.'

I was curious about how this affected Carol's relationships. 'What happened with the singles leader you acted obnoxiously toward?'

'During this process our friendship blossomed. I stopped testing her commitment, and that enabled me to relax in her company. Eventually, her business transferred her to the east coast. I was very sad, but not devastated. My life didn't crumble with her departure.'

As Carol continued to trust in God, she gained a clearer vision of those around her. 'Because I was rooted in my relationship with the Lord, I didn't saddle my friends with such high expectations any more. They didn't have to meet all my needs. I found a new freedom in relationships when I finally realised that my friends would make mistakes, break commitments and fail in their efforts. This gave me a new perspective on forgiveness too. Because my existence didn't depend on my friends, I actually sensed a greater freedom, and was truly able to forgive them unconditionally, just as God forgives me.'

Carol is certainly not the only woman to have struggled with fears of abandonment. If you have difficulty in trusting God to prove himself faithful, take heart. Listen to what Psalm 27:9–10 says: 'Don't forsake me, O God of my salvation. For if my father and mother should abandon me, you would welcome and comfort me' (TLB).

No longer do you have to fear abandonment or try to find comfort in yourself. Jehovah is there for you, standing with his arms wide open, ready to receive you.

God the Father and Jesus are united

Sometimes we make the mistake of thinking that we can coerce God the Father into a decision by appealing to Jesus to 'put in a good word' for us! If this is our mindset, we have overlooked Hebrews 1:3, which says: 'The Son is the radiance of God's glory and the exact representation of his being.'

It is not a question of God being the stern, unloving father and Jesus being the likable, approachable brother figure to whom God the Father listens. In Isaiah 49:15 God tells of his love for us: 'Can a mother forget the baby at her breast and have no compassion on the child she has borne? Though she may forget, I will not forget you! *See, I have engraved you on the palms of my hands...*' (italics mine).

Christ's love for us was also engraved onto his hands through his crucifixion. The scars from the nails serve as a lasting reminder of the love of God. An awesome thought.

One day, back in North Wales, a simple notion had a profound affect on me. *Every time I read a characteristic of Jesus, I am in fact reading a description of God!* So, when I read in Matthew 9:36 about Jesus, I was seeing a description of God's character. 'When he saw the crowds, he had compassion on them, because they were harassed and helpless, like sheep without a shepherd.'

Our God is not an unknown God, but he is loving,

forgiving, gentle, courageous, confrontive and longsuffer-
ing. With this understanding, I sensed the gap between
God and me beginning to close.

Priorities

As women seeking freedom from lesbianism, we must
establish a right focus. It is easy to concentrate on healing
to the detriment of our relationship with Jesus Christ. We
desire healing, but we need Jesus. Our deepest need is to
establish a relationship with him. Healing then comes as a
by-product of this, and not the other way around.

Carol also shared a problem she encountered early on in
her healing process. It highlights the distinction between
what we desire and what we need. 'When I first joined a
church, it particularly irritated me to find men seemed to
run the show. My past dealings with the opposite sex had
been less than favourable up to that point!'

'So what did you do?' I asked.

'I resolved to overcome my attitude towards men as
soon as possible so that I could fully enter into church life.'

'That seems reasonable enough,' I interjected.

'Well, it was in theory,' Carol continued, 'but I became
so engrossed in this issue that I failed to experience the love
of Jesus. I really hadn't understood God's methods of
healing. I didn't realise my need to receive from Jesus. I
guess I had an incorrect understanding of Christianity
altogether.'

God is a gentleman—he does not force healing on his
children. Carol desired to 'sort out her problems with
men'. However, in reality she needed to let Jesus take
charge over her healing process. Only after much effort
and frustration on her part did Carol finally give up her
quest—her agenda—and let Jesus' love woo her into healing.

A difficulty arises when we confuse our desires and our

needs. We may desire freedom from homosexuality, or desire to have a husband and family, but our real need is to find God and to know him in his fullness. Leanne Payne deals with this concept in her book, *The Broken Image*.

> Knowing that Jesus is truly Emmanuel, God with us, and learning to practice his Presence is vital to being healed and remaining healed. This practice of the Presence is not a method, but a walk with a Person—and in this walk there is always healing.[1]

As well as having a personal knowledge of Jesus, we need to fill ourselves with the truth of the Bible. However, it is important not only to read God's Word, but to allow it to change our lives. We are to be doers of the Word, and that can only happen as we believe what is written. This is where the Holy Spirit comes in.

The Holy Spirit: God working behind the scene

If a knowledge of the word were enough to get us through life's struggles, Jesus would not have told his disciples to wait in Jerusalem for the empowering of the Holy Spirit (Acts 1:4–5).

Without the Holy Spirit to teach us and help us apply truth in our lives, the Bible would be a lifeless, historical manuscript. Similarly, without the Holy Spirit, our Christian walk would be lacklustre and barren. We would bear little resemblance to the 'on fire' believers in the early church.

The Holy Spirit is the third person in the Trinity. Jesus describes the Spirit's role to his disciples as follows: 'But when he, the Spirit of truth, comes, he will guide you into all truth. He will not speak on his own; he will speak only what he hears, and he will tell you what is yet to come' (Jn 16:13).

Beside teaching and guiding us, God's Holy Spirit plays

a crucial role in our healing process. He prompts us regarding the directions we need to take in seeking God. Not only does he walk us through the growth process, he comforts us through the trying times. 'If you love me, obey me; and I will ask the Father and he will give you another Comforter, and *he will never leave you*' (Jn 14:15–16), TLB, italics mine).

We need not run to the regrigerator or another person's arms when the going gets tough and healing seems a long way off. God has already supplied the one true Comforter. 'No, I will not abandon you or leave you as orphans—I will come to you' (Jn 14:18, TLB).

As women who have entrusted ourselves to God— Father, Son and Spirit—we are no longer orphans or slaves. We are daughters in God's family, and can live in freedom.

We are free women

At this moment you may not feel like a free woman. Perhaps you feel bound up by your emotions and your circumstances. While it is important to assess your current situation and validate the way that you feel, it is very important to take hold as truth what the Bible has to say.

'We know that our old self was crucified with him so that the sinful body might be destroyed, and we might no longer be enslaved to sin' (Rom 6:6, RSV).

We may be living as slaves, but God has proclaimed freedom through the death and resurrection of his Son. As our understanding of God grows, we will be able to walk in the freedom that God makes available.

And who is God? Father, Son and Spirit. Creator, source of life, sustainer of life, rewarder, the ultimate lover, the One who will never leave us or let us down.

Those thoughts are amazing enough in themselves. But as I continue receiving God's love and growing in his word, I find an even deeper revelation. As Christians, God is not only our Master and Saviour—he is our true parent.

For your information

The Bible records many different names for God. Just a few of his Hebrew names are El Shaddai, Adonai, Jehovah, Elohim and El Elyon. Each reveals something unique about God's character and how he relates to his people.

Most versions of the Old Testament use LORD (printed all in capital letters) to translate the Hebrew name, Jehovah. The word Lord (only capital 'L') is used to translate Adonai, which means 'master'.

You may find a study on the names of God quite rewarding. I recommend *Names of God* by Nathan Stone (Moody Press) as a good introductory study.

For further study

1. *The Pursuit of God* by A W Tozer (STL: UK, 1987).
2. *Your God is Too Small* by J B Phillips (Macmillan Publishing Co: USA, 1961). Phillips covers various misconceptions of who God is.
3. *Names of God* by Nathan Stone (Moody Press: USA, 1944).
4. *The Broken Image: Restoring Personal Wholeness Through Healing Prayer* by Leanne Payne (Crossway Books: USA, 1981) (UK edition: Kingsway Publications, 1988).

CHAPTER THREE

GOD, OUR TRUE PARENT

Genesis 1:27 informs us that God possesses all female and male attributes. He is as loving, compassionate, and tender as he is firm, upright, and powerful. It is the balance between his feminine and masculine characteristics that enables God to be the perfect parental role model. He is the perfect combination of the mother and father.

In this chapter, there is more emphasis placed on God's role as father. Many women in the process of overcoming lesbianism need a new, correct image of God the Father so that further healing can take place.

Our miscast portraits of God

Tessa, a counsellee, came from an abusive home. Although her frail, waif-like features concealed a considerable inner strength, her father's violent outbursts had left Tessa often cautious and fearful. During a counselling session one day, I asked Tessa to read Isaiah 40:11. I hoped to counteract fears stemming from her father and show how God the Father loved her. 'He tends His flock like a shepherd: He gathers the lambs in his arms and carries them close to his heart; he gently leads those that have young.'

Tessa laughed after she read this passage. 'I don't believe it,' she smiled. But her smile could not hide the pain she really felt. Although her voice said she didn't believe, her eyes said, 'I want to believe, but I can't.' She loved God, but she could not trust him. As with her father, Tessa feared intimacy with God, anticipating he would hurt her if she ever let him get too close.

As children, most of us develop false and exaggerated portraits of God, based on interactions we had with our father. Dad was the 'mould' into which we try to stuff God the Father.

Here are a number of typical misconceptions of God found among people of various backgrounds. As you read through the list, you may deduce that your father does not fit under any of the headings, or that he is a combination of one or two of the following categories.

God, the weak wimp

This misconception is based on a father who avoids responsibility and conflict. He rarely takes the leadership role in the home, but depends on his wife to run the show. The father lacks discipline, and has an immature outlook. He is given to inconsistency and laziness. He tends to be insecure, and can be overly emotional or emotionally absent. Based on this role model, the daughter sees God as distant, ineffectual and weak.

God, the abusive boxer

The earthly father is physically or emotionally abusive. He is stubborn, rude and angry in his interaction with others. He can be given to alcohol abuse, which invites temper tantrums and violence. The father sabotages everything and everyone he perceives as a threat to him. He verbally cuts people down to size, and uses shame as an effective weapon. The daughter sees God as mean-spirited, untrustworthy and someone to avoid.

God, the silent vacationer

This misunderstanding of God is based on a dad who is emotionally or physically absent from the home. This means that he fails to take an active interest in the affairs of his family. The daughter perceives God as someone who does not listen, does not talk, and does not show affection. He is uninvolved in her life.

God, the harsh judge

The girl makes this conclusion based on a dad who is demanding, a perfectionist and tends to be a workaholic. The father often resents his wife and children, and has a tendency to isolate himself from his family. The dad accepts no responsibility for wrongdoing, and shows conditional love—that is, dependent on what they do—to his children. His focus is toward success and materialism rather than relationships. The father intimidates, holds grudges and is strictly unforgiving. The daughter sees God as ruling with an iron fist, showing no mercy or compassion.

God, the clinging controller

The earthly father is often described as someone who smothers those around him under the guise of 'love' and concern. He controls and manipulates others, showering them with material goods and attention. He is intense, demanding, over-protective and does not let others make their own decisions and mistakes. The daughter sees God as mushy, sickeningly sweet and out to run her life.

Separating images of God from images of Dad

It took time for Tessa to fully appreciate that God and her father were not one and the same person. Although her father had been abusive, God shows compassion. Although her father was harsh, God displays kindness. Although her father was judgemental, God overflows with mercy and grace.

At the close of one particular counselling session, Tessa prayed a prayer of repentance. 'Father, I acknowledge my sin against you. I have chosen to believe my own thoughts about you, based on circumstances and people around me. Please forgive me. Change my vision of you—give me spiritual eyes so that I can see you clearly. I release any anger and wrong expectations I have had of you, and I welcome any change you want to make in my life.'

After Tessa had finished praying, I invited God to reveal himself to her as we waited quietly for his response. For the first time ever, Tessa sensed God's deep love and concern for her as she envisioned herself sitting contentedly on his knee.

As Tessa left my office, I reflected on perceptions I held of my own father. They were hazy and unformed. I pondered how my non-emotional relationship with dad influenced my relationship with God. I recognised that any problems I had with authority did not necessarily originate in my relationship with dad alone. The mother/father input combination formed my thinking in that area. But I knew that my feelings toward Dad certainly coloured my response to God.

What was your earthly father like? Were there times when he said one thing and did something else? Could you rely on your daddy at all times? Were there times when he made promises that he was unable to keep?

I have found it reassuring to know that God is not dishonest or scheming or unreliable. He is just and upright in all that he does.

'God is not a man, that he should lie, nor a son of man, that he should change his mind. Does he speak and then not act? Does he promise and not fulfill?' (Num 23:19).

True parenting—the Lord is trustworthy

The Israelites knew that their God was powerful. He had manifested his awesome power in Egypt with signs and wonders, finally convincing Pharaoh exactly who was boss.

As the Israelites packed up their belongings, certain questions must have nagged them. *Will God look after me? How long will the journey take? Will I make it? What does he expect of me?* They needed confidence in Jehovah Jireh, a title of God which means 'The LORD will provide'.

Not only did Jehovah show Israel he was all powerful, but after calling them into the wilderness, he proved himself to be both dependable and worthy of their trust. Jehovah never left them.

By day the LORD went ahead of them in a pillar of cloud to guide them on their way and by night in a pillar of fire to give them light, so that they could travel by day or night. *Neither the pillar of cloud by day nor the pillar of fire by night left its place in front of the people* (Ex 13:21–22, italics mine).

Taking the story of the exodus as a whole, dependency on God certainly did not happen immediately for the Hebrews.

Many of us have difficulty in trusting God to be in front and behind us at all times. As we examine God's provision for the Hebrews, allow God to show his love and care to you through these examples.

True parenting—God protects and shields us

In 1 Corinthians 13:8, God tells us that 'love never fails'. He also tells us in 1 John 4:18 that 'perfect love drives out fear'. In his perfect love for us, the Lord extends protection, discipline, warmth and encouragement, among many other things. We see God's protection toward his people in Exodus 14:19–20: 'Then the angel of God, who had been travelling in front of Israel's army, withdrew and went behind them. The pillar of cloud also moved from in front and stood behind them, coming between the armies of Egypt and Israel.'

In this instance God chose to deliver the Israelites. Other times, he told them to fight their enemies. Our deliverance from lesbianism is somewhat similar.

Often God chooses to place himself between us and our temptations.

I had been a Christian for six months when my ex-lover visited from Australia. For three days I resisted all temptations to have sex with her. In reality I knew that it was merely a question of time before I fell. We were to be alone together for seven weeks. Because no one knew of my struggles, I had no support team to pray with me and help me through this testing time. If only I had spoken to someone, perhaps the seemingly inevitable might not have happened. But the word accountable did not enter my 'personal Christian dictionary' until three years later!

The sexual part of the relationship was mixed with mental anguish, guilt, sorrow and a desire to get right with God. I hated what I was doing, but felt unable to battle and resist my 'natural' desires.

Then, one day, just as I was in the process of falling yet

again, I called on the name of the Lord. 'God, no!' I yelled inside my head.

Immediately, I felt a barrier come between us. It arrived so fast and powerfully, I sensed it had been launched from heaven! At once, the lust and desire disappeared. I was able to get out of the bed, get dressed, apologise and leave the room. Other temptations followed, but I knew that God had placed himself between us.

True parenting—God asks us to act responsibly

God does not always choose to place himself between us and our temptations.

At other times the Lord calls us to stand and fight, but this does not mean that he loves us any less.

Every September parents wave farewell to their children as they send them off to college. Did they suddenly stop loving their kids, which prompted this departure? Certainly not. I am sure that many parents ache when their offspring leave home. But they recognise how necessary this move is if the children are to mature into responsible adults. Their children have to learn to stand in the world and make decisions for themselves. Releasing them does not mean that the parents have emotionally abandoned the kids either. Most parents are only a phone call away, ready to assist their children where possible.

God releases us in a similar way so we can grow into mature adults. We are not abandoned. Instead, he oversees our walk and is available whenever we seek him.

God not only calls us to stand and fight, sometimes we have to kneel too!

I remember once experiencing such overwhelming sexual temptation that I remained on my knees until one o'clock in the morning, reading 1 Corinthians 6:11, which says homosexuals can change: 'And that is what some of you were. But you were washed, you were sanctified, you were justified in the name of the Lord Jesus Christ and by the Spirit of our God.'

My mind, emotions and body screamed for sexual comfort from a woman, but I knew that I must stand my ground based on God's word. I had soaked the page with my tears, but as I arose that night, I knew that a battle had been won in the spiritual realm.

Even if we can only find one verse in the whole of the Bible to keep us from falling, then we must cling to it. Whatever situation faces us, we can be assured that God provides abundant care and protection.

> But remember this—the wrong desires that come into your life aren't anything new and different. Many others have faced exactly the same problems before you. *And no temptation is irresistible.* You can trust God to keep the temptation from becoming so strong that you can't stand up against it, for he has promised this and will do what he says (1 Cor 10:13, TLB, italics mine).

God as our true parent is not only concerned with the spiritual aspect of our lives, but he is also interested in the more mundane facets of our existence.

True parenting—God continually cares for us

The Lord's continual care for the Israelites extended beyond protection, too. He met their physical needs. '...At twilight you will eat meat, and in the morning you will be filled with bread. Then you will know that I am the LORD your God' (Ex 16:12).

God has never had a problem expressing his love for his people, whether toward the nation of Israel back then or toward us, his children, today.

In my own life, I have found that he often uses many people around me to show his kindness and love. His love shines through their acts of kindness, sense of humour, giving, or just being there when I need a sounding board. 'When Israel was a child, I loved him, and out of Egypt I called My son.... *I led them with cords of human kindness, with ties of love*' (Hos 11:1, 4, italics mine).

Luke 13:34 also shows God's tenderness toward us. 'O Jerusalem, Jerusalem, you who kill the prophets and stone those sent to you, how often I have longed to gather you together, *as a hen gathers her chicks under her wings*, but you were not willing!' (italics mine).

A hen protects her chicks from the rain, cold, wind and scorching heat. She is there to fight off any thing or any one that would cause them harm. The chicks remain safe, provided they stay close to their mother. Likewise, God desires to protect us from outside forces. We can run and be safe under the shelter of his wing.

True parenting and our past experience

God's parenting involves not only power and authority, but also care and nurturing. Human parents should follow his pattern. They should give selflessly. Godly parents should provide security and consistency and deal predictably with their offspring. They should openly express their thoughts and feelings toward their children in a loving way. Also important is for them to give accurate, affirmative feedback to their children in order to establish their sense of worth.

Sadly, for so many of us, our experience cannot be likened to God's idea of what a parent should be. For some of us, the words *parent* and *family* do not evoke cosy fireside memories. Rather, they elicit fear, resentment, repulsion and anger. Unfortunately, many of our negative images of father, and parents in general, hinder our walk with God. Many of us coming out of a lesbian lifestyle find ourselves unable to fully embrace all that he has to give us. This is due to our deep lack of trust and our gnawing sense of worthlessness stemming from our childhood.

As for most people, coming to terms with my relationship with my own parents has not been easy. I am very grateful to the Reverend Gordon Dalbey for a sermon which helped me grasp the truth of God as my true parent. Some of his concepts appear in the following section.

True parenting — God's original design

God originally designed for our parents to exhibit the qualities and characteristics of himself. A newborn baby girl, if capable of logical reasoning, would consider her parents to be God. She would look at her parents and deduce the following:

1. I am created in their image.
2. I am dependent on them.
3. They are all powerful.
4. They provide for me.
5. They protect me.

Parents should guide their daughter into gradually separating herself from themselves, and into recognising that her parents are actually incapable of fulfilling her original expectations. Continual parental instruction enables the child to transfer her list of expectations onto God, and grow up to lead a functional, godly life.

God's plan breaks down due to the parents' own spiritual brokenness and personal problems. In the vast majority of families, there has been some flaw in the system. For a few families, the breakdown is minor. For others, abuse, violence, alcohol, divorce and a myriad of other disasters, devastate family life.

It is out of that background that the daughter alters the above list in ways like those shown overleaf.

1. I am created in their image. *I don't like my parents' image. I am my own person. My identity is unique, and I will separate myself from anyone else's influence.*
2. I am dependent on them. *I don't need my parents. I am a capable person. I will run my own life.*
3. They are all powerful. *They may use violence and verbal abuse to 'keep me in line', but I will not let that affect me.*
4. They provide for me. *They don't provide for me the way I want. I will get what I want. I will provide for myself.*
5. They protect me. *They don't protect me. I don't trust them, or anyone else. I'm the only one I can trust, so I'll look after myself.*

The daughter makes an inappropriate transference of expectations onto God, based on faulty parenting. She sees him through the same lens as she sees her parents. She pulls herself away from God, just as she did from her parents.

Consequently, the daughter is unable to receive from God all the blessings he has for her. Her self-protective defence system means that she will more readily rely on self than on God. She will see his power as a threat rather than a blessing, and will view herself as her own need-meeter rather than relying upon God's provision.

A new start—the light goes on!

One day I shared with Susan, a counsellee, these concepts about God's original intent for parenting. Her relationship with both parents had really discouraged her. Susan drew her long legs onto the armchair and rested her chin on her knees.

'You're not alone in this,' I told her. 'We all have imperfect parents, and their attitudes and actions affect how we end up viewing God.'

Susan looked confused. 'I guess that sounds reasonable. But how can I break out of that? I feel like a prisoner.'

I went on to explain God's provision for us to correct

our false images of him. 'The process begins when we receive the gift of salvation. Being born again breaks us from bondages to the past and our flawed, earthly parents, and links us to God, our true and perfect parent.'

Flipping to John chapter 1 in my Amplified Bible, where it talks about becoming children of God, I asked Susan to read John 1:13 aloud: 'Who owe their birth neither to bloods, nor to the will of the flesh [that of physical impulse], *nor to the will of man [that of a natural father], but to God*— They are born of God!' (italics mine).

When she had finished reading, she put my Bible back on my desk. I rested my hand on my Bible. 'Susan, does this passage answer your question about breaking free from the past? As we incorporate this truth into our lives, we're freed up to believe all that the Bible says regarding the attributes of God our Father. Whatever image of God we may be carrying because of our own earthly father need not hinder us any longer.'

Susan sat bolt upright in her chair. 'Wow,' she exclaimed, 'that's amazing! I really do have a second chance. I can start over again.'

Susan's views on God and parents

Susan and I had many discussions before about her view of God and his role in her life, but we made very little progress. When it came to believing that God was attentive to her, Susan would shake her head. 'Not me,' she would mumble, running her fingers through her short auburn hair. 'When I pray, my prayers get no higher than the ceiling. God's not there for me.' Considering her upbringing, it wasn't surprising to see how Susan had reached her conclusions.

'I guess to an outsider, our family looked like an average American household. My parents didn't fight, get drunk or cause a stir in the neighbourhood.'

In fact, nothing about Susan's family distinguished them in the least bit from any other household in the neighbourhood. However, her parents had long since ceased to relate to each other. Now they were merely biding their time until the children grew up and left home. After they had fulfilled their parental duties, they would file for divorce.

'My parents provided everything we could possibly want in a material sense. My brothers and I never went hungry or lacked clothes. But I was desperate for my parents just to say they loved me. It almost seemed like these words were taboo.'

It was not hard to see how Susan had been starved of nurture and care—the household appeared emotionally cold and lifeless. No one acknowledged difficulties, let alone discussed them.

Years earlier, Susan's father had abdicated his responsibility as head of the household. He wandered somewhere between work and the television set, taking little interest in the activities and pursuits of his children. Susan longed to please her dad, but all efforts, even getting high results at school, did little to rouse him.

Her mother had assumed a matriarchal role. She doled out the discipline along with the dinner in an attempt to keep some semblance of order in this household which included two teenage sons. To the neighbours, she looked like the model housewife—modern and efficient. But to Susan, she seemed more like a stranger—cold and aloof.

Making inner vows

During one counselling session, Susan recalled a particular incident from when she was twelve years old. 'Dad had assumed his usual position, sitting in the living room armchair, while the rest of us sat around the kitchen table, eating dinner.

'Mum reprimanded Matthew, my fifteen-year-old brother, for some minor incident. I don't even remember what it was. But Matt turned on Mum in a rage. He was so abusive! He screamed at her things like, "I hate you. You're always on my case! You don't really care about me. You just want to control me like you do Dad." Then my Mum broke down and cried.'

I suspected this event held a key to why Susan had become vulnerable to homosexual struggles. I knew I needed to push her a little more so we could explore the connection. 'How did you feel after Matt said that to your mother?'

'It was awful, Jeanette. Because what Matt said were the exact same things I'd thought myself. I was so disgusted with her. She was like a robot—do everything right and put out a good image for the neighbours. I hated that, but I wanted her to love me too. And then I guess I thought, *If this is what being a woman is all about, you can keep it!*'

'And what was going on with your dad right then?'

'I glanced over at my father, but he was just staring at the television, oblivious to this uproar in the kitchen. Typical Dad. Ignore Matt, ignore Mum, ignore me.'

Gently I asked, 'Susan, what were you thinking about your dad?'

With tears in her eyes, Susan reflected on the resolution she had made so many years ago. 'I remember thinking, *You creep! I don't care if you ever decide to love me, because I don't want it. I don't need you. I'll take care of myself.*'

During the past nine years, even as a Christian, Susan tried to find love her own way. Because of her vows toward her dad, she had dismissed all men as being of little value to her life and had sought out sexual relationships with women to fill her deep longing to be special to someone.

Renouncing the vows

For Susan, some major roots of her involvement in lesbianism were beginning to emerge. Two weeks later we explored other areas of her life during a counselling session.

It became apparent that Susan had rejected much of her feminine identity. She realised that she viewed her mother as an ineffectual person. Susan had decided that such an image was not for her. In fact, she had wanted to distance herself from as much of her feminine identity as possible. Coupled with the poor male role model shown by her father, Susan had become very confused as to her own gender identity. 'I just don't feel as though I fit in,' she confessed to me. 'I know I'm not a man, but I don't feel like a real woman either. What am I—a third sex?'

'Identity is a very important issue, Susan, and we certainly will consider that sometime soon. But for right now, I feel like something else is blocking your progress.' Susan had been trying to follow God for the past year and was making very slow headway. Now seemed the right moment to work through the subject we had opened two weeks earlier.

'Remember when we discussed your inner vows? Susan, the time has come to renounce those vows,' I shared. 'You are born again of a new parent. You don't have to live under the confinement of the old system.'

Together we reviewed what Susan talked about in her last counselling session, and how inner vows are a form of self-protection. We discussed how, as children, we sometimes see such vows as necessary in order to minimise further emotional hurt to ourselves. But I also pointed out how they obstruct our relationship with God.

'If we are still protecting ourselves, Susan, we are preventing God from taking care of us. You need to renounce those vows, including your thoughts on not wanting to be a woman.'

As we prayed, Susan openly renounced the vows she had made as the hurting twelve-year-old girl. 'Thank you, God, that you are my real father. Even though my dad didn't seem to care at all about me, I accept your word that you do care about me and love me. I also thank you for caring and loving me as a mother should.'

She paused, obviously struggling. 'Thank you for making me a woman. I don't really know yet what that even means. But in faith, I accept that you have made me female, and I welcome all that you have for me as a woman of God. I also renounce my vow to be self-sufficient. I acknowledge that you will supply all my needs if I let you. Jesus, I welcome you to fill the role as provider of my physical, emotional and spiritual needs.'

Susan relaxed in the armchair, flung her arms over the sides and heaved a sigh of relief.

Pursuing God's way

In the Bible, the word *repent* means a turning *from* our sins and simultaneously turning *toward* the Lord. Leaving lesbianism behind is not just a question of renouncing the old, but of replacing our faulty methods of survival with God's pattern for living. We have to accept what the Bible says about God's tender heart toward us. I know this is a struggle when we have spent many years believing lies about God and ourselves.

For Susan and for Tessa, who also dealt with an unhealthy home life when growing up, the healing process took time. They had to surrender themselves into the care and protection of the Lord. Also, both women had to acknowledge and explore the roots of their lesbianism in order to receive greater healing. But it did come over time, just as it will for you as you continue to pursue God's way.

For further study

1. *The Father Heart of God* by Floyd McClung (Kingsway Publications: UK, 1985) (US edition: Harvest House, 1985).
2. *The Blessing* by Gary Smalley and John Trent (Thomas Nelson: USA, 1986) (UK edition: Word, 1989).

Slavery and Release
From Bondage

CHAPTER FOUR

ROOTS, SHOOTS AND FRUITS

Is lesbianism a form of slavery?

Some Christian women see their homosexuality as bondage. They find certain compensations from living as a lesbian, but underneath that superficial security, many live a life of despair. Since these women are Christians while still actively pursuing lesbianism, their conscience bothers them at some point. They never really want to be imprisoned by their lesbian identity 'taskmaster'. Release from this slavery comes with rejoicing.

Other Christian women do not see homosexuality as bondage. Entering into the lifestyle brings exhilarating pay-offs—pleasure, power, sisterhood and some sense of intimacy. For these women, the lesbian identity seems to bring freedom and relief. So their choice to leave comes strictly out of obedience to God, and not because they hate the homosexual way of life.

Many women who want to leave lesbianism behind do not fit neatly into either of these two groups. Perhaps they alternate between liking the lifestyle and being frustrated with it.

In all these cases, I believe the women actually are

slaves, whether fully realising that or not. They are bound to the roots of lesbianism—their ingrained responses to past events and subsequent emotions—which lead to their current attitudes and actions.

The first time Jesus spoke in public ministry, he promised freedom for those in slavery. That includes those of us who desire to leave lesbianism behind.

'The Spirit of the Lord is upon me; he has appointed me to preach Good News to the poor; he has sent me to heal the brokenhearted and to announce that captives shall be released and the blind shall see, that the downtrodden shall be freed from their oppressors, and that God is ready to give blessings to all who come to him' (Lk 4:18–19, TLB).

For some of us, the thought of being released from this slavery is a frightening prospect. Up to this point we may never have experienced freedom. We may have spent a lifetime believing that 'I was born this way.' To challenge and overcome our slave mentality requires that we look into our past, assess people and situations in our life both then and now, and desire for now and the future to follow God—whatever lies ahead.

What am I up against?

Tessa strode into the room and sat on the edge of my desk.

I put down my glasses and leaned back in my chair. Obviously, Tessa meant business.

'I want answers,' she demanded.

'Answers?' I asked. 'About what?'

She sighed deeply and shrugged her shoulders. It appeared I was asking unnecessary questions. 'I need to know why I do what I do. Give me something concrete so that I know what I'm up against. I need to know factors that have influenced me. If I know them, then maybe I can tackle them.'

I understood Tessa's frustration. She was tired of pummelling air and wanted something tangible to work on. She desired answers to some very pertinent questions.

'Where do you want to start?' I settled down for a long session.

What exactly is lesbianism?

Tessa jumped right in. 'I know what I've been doing for the last few years, but I still couldn't really explain lesbianism in one short sentence if anyone asked me. Can you?'

I thought for a moment. 'No! That's because the term lesbianism covers three categories of women. First are those women who strive to fulfil sexual desires and emotional needs through other women. The second group have not acted out sexually, but have sought completion through an emotional relationship with another woman. The third category of lesbians are those who were too frightened to act upon their desires, so they resort to fantasy. All three types of women have a primary yearning to find completion of self—a sense of wholeness—within real or imagined relationships with other women.'

'Well,' Tessa said, 'I'm one of those who did act out sexually.' A puzzled look crossed her face. 'But that doesn't explain why I did it. Was I born this way?'

'No,' I shook my head. 'The Bible makes it perfectly clear in Genesis chapters one to three that God created us male and female, for the purpose of relating to the opposite sex in a spiritual, emotional, and physical way. God would have embraced homosexuality and said so in Scripture if that was in his plan. However, we see quite the opposite—that he actually condemns homosexual activity. God wouldn't create us with homosexual thoughts and desires, and then turn around and condemn us for having them! That's not within the character of a just God.'

Tessa nodded slowly. 'Okay, I think I understand.

Sometimes I still have trouble agreeing wholeheartedly with God because loving someone just seems so right—even if it's another woman. However, I'm learning to agree with him even if I don't—if you know what I mean!' Tessa grinned at me.

I did get her meaning. I had gone through the same struggle myself.

Tessa continued, 'So—if I wasn't born gay, where do I go from here?'

She seemed ready for the next step. 'Well, let's look at roots,' I smiled and pulled some diagrams out of my desk drawer. 'Roots and shoots and fruit.'

A seed planted in soil

I sorted through the stack, then pointed to the paper I wanted to use first.

'I know this will be a bit abstract, Tessa. But we'll apply these principles to some real situations as we go through these diagrams. That will help make it practical. Another time we can go into depth on five major roots of lesbianism:

1. the relationship between mother and daughter,
2. the relationship between father and daughter,
3. the dysfunctional family,
4. peer influence,
5. traumatic events.'

'All right. I've been waiting to hear this stuff!' Tessa flopped into the chair next to me, pulling her notebook and pen from her back-pack. 'Ready when you are.'

I began with Diagram 1. 'Let's start with the first picture here. When you're born, it's like you are a seed planted in the soil. The soil represents the environment you're in—all those things around you that you really don't have any control over. Such as being born into an alcoholic, single-

Diagram 1

parent or abusive family. Perhaps the dad here is passive and the mum is domineering.

'This "soil" environment would also cover all kinds of victimisation—things that happen to you that you don't have much control over.'

Tessa leaned forward and looked at me intently. 'Like being sexually abused?' she asked.

'Right.' I nodded. 'That could be a very sad part of a girl's environment while growing up. Another type of victimisation could happen if people accidentally calling you 'Sonny' because they mistakenly thought you were a boy. Perhaps your siblings picked on you all the time. Or your schoolmates purposely called you names, like *butch* or *lesbo*.'

'Ooh!' Tessa grimaced. I had hit a sore spot with the name-calling examples.

'Those taunting nicknames the kids at school called you really hurt, didn't they?'

Tessa bit her lip, looked out of the window, and nodded slightly.

'I'm sorry you ever experienced that, Tess. But your reaction just now to those painful memories is an important concept to examine as part of these diagrams we're looking at.'

Your reactions create your roots

I pulled out the next picture in the 'Tree Series', as I had come to call it.

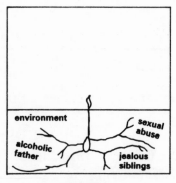

Diagram 2

'Now, for Diagram 2. As with any seed, you're going to react to your environment. You take in nutrients and poisons from the soil around you, and your seed puts out roots.

'And you do have control over your roots, because those are your reactions over a period of time to what's in the soil.'

I decided to apply Tessa's example to these concepts.

'If a man sexually abused you as a child, that's an event you couldn't control. You were a victim.

'But your reaction toward that molestation helps dictate how the tree will grow.

'As the root grows over time, it supports a shoot that eventually becomes the tree trunk. The shoot shapes the general condition of the trunk, which then determines the kind of fruit you'll be able to grow on your tree. Ultimately, roots strongly influence your crop of fruit.'

I put down the sheet and asked Tessa if the illustration was clear.

'I see,' she said slowly, glancing over the diagrams again. 'I'm following you so far.'

Three types of reaction patterns

I shuffled through my papers and pulled out a chart. 'Okay, then let me bring in this chart about types of root reactions to such events. In my view, root reactions involve three parts, which tend to happen consecutively. First come the cognitive or thinking responses. Second, the emotional or feeling responses. And third, the behavioural or action responses.'

I paused and Tessa said, 'Okay, I think I'm clear on that—think, feel and act.'

'Great. Now, as I see it there are three basic types of reaction patterns: denial, blame and healthy. Exploring these patterns is important to find healing in one's root structure.'

Re-sponse	Reaction Syndromes		
	Cognitive (Thinking)	Emotional (Feeling)	Behavioural (Action)
Denial	Repression: The event was so painful that the memory is hidden. Minimisation: The victim acknowledges the event, but acts as though it was not as traumatic as it truly was.	Emotional shutdown: Victim internalises feelings instead of expresses them.	No action taken towards healing.

Blame	Victim is aware of the event, acknowledges damage was done, and knows the perpetrator. Tendency to over-generalise.	Overt anger, rage, contempt, bitterness, hatred, etc.	Revenge channel anger into unhealthy relationships, etc.
Health-iness	Victim acknowledges the damage, and chooses the route of healing and forgiveness.	Recognises the emotions and confusion, but yields them to the Holy Spirit for help in sorting them through.	Takes concrete steps toward personal healing, forgiving the perpetrator and, if appropriate, to initiate reconciliation.

Reaction pattern 1: denial

I covered up the bottom portion of the chart so we could focus on the top third.

'Let's continue with the sexual abuse example and work it through. First we'll apply the think, feel and act parts to the denial pattern. Denial means you treat something as if it really isn't there. You disavow it or refuse to face it.

'In the case of childhood sexual abuse, it is so emotionally painful that some girls who were victims deny the very existence of the abuse. Or they may not even remember it. That's called repressing the memory. Or they might acknowledge the abuse happened, but minimise its effects. So, in the denial mode, cognitive reactions to the abuse could be either:

Abused? Not me. No one abused me. I don't have that problem. (Repression), or,

Abused? Me. Oh, something happened a long time ago. But it really wasn't anything major. (Minimisation)

Tessa winced. 'How could you not know that you were abused?'

'Unfortunately, it's quite a common occurrence. Something like seventy to eighty per cent of people who have been abused in childhood go through a period of repression. The event is so traumatic that, for some girls, the only way to cope is to submerge the memory of it. Although these painful memories don't hurt us in a conscious sense, many of those girls grow up with vague reminders, such as scary dreams. Often these dreams revolve around someone chasing them and the girl can't escape, or encounters with snakes.'

'You know, Jeanette,' Tessa gasped, 'I know somebody that has recurring dreams like that!'

I wanted Tessa to have hope, whether for herself or her friend—whoever had been sexually abused. 'Sexual abuse and incest are difficult issues to deal with. But many women who were violated sexually do come to a point where God, in his grace, allows the memories to surface and be worked through.'

We sat in silence for a moment. Tessa needed time to process this information. When she seemed ready to move on, I continued with the chart. 'After the repression or minimising comes the emotional shut-down. For instance, you might unconsciously be aware that a man hurt you and you feel like this.'

I don't hate men. I'm just totally indifferent toward them. I don't need them.

'Your actions in the denial mode would actually be inaction—you wouldn't deal with the issues involved.'

I don't see the need to do anything. I'm okay. Really!

I looked my client right in the eyes. 'You see, Tessa, the

hurt still exists underneath, even if you haven't dealt with the facts, feelings or resulting actions. The reality is that the abuse still affects you. The internalised hurt can come out in various ways, perhaps in headaches, stress, fear, panic attacks, depression or eating disorders. Maybe you'll distance yourself from God, or avoid any kind of emotional closeness with men. Sometimes women do end up in a relationship with a man, but spend the rest of their lives avoiding intimacy. When someone has been so violated, it's often hard to define where you end and other people begin. In other words, it's hard to set boundaries and say, "*No*." '

'Wow!' Tessa exclaimed. 'If for no other reason, I guess that's basis enough to work through this issue! Especially if it means stopping others from taking advantage of you again.'

Reaction pattern 2: blame

'That's an excellent point.' Next I uncovered the second portion of the chart.

'Another basic type of reaction pattern is blame. Here you acknowledge that the abuse took place, but your thinking takes a completely different twist than in the denial pattern.'

I feel used and it's his fault. I hate him for what he's done. I'm justified in hating him.

'Overgeneralising is common in the blame mode, Tessa. That means you make a broad conclusion based on just one or a few cases. Because you hate the man who abused you, your logic when you overgeneralise might look like this: *A man abused me. Therefore all men are abusive. I hate the man who abused me, therefore I reject all men.* That's exactly what many sexually abused women do. They end up hating all the men in the world.'

Just look at me—I was robbed of my childhood. I have total contempt for the man who abused me. And all men are just like him. I hate them all!

'Attitudes result in actions. You may end up no longer being open to respond to men, but just react to them through your own veil of bitterness. Any trust you may have had towards a man has long since disappeared, and you are left with you defending yourself. Thus, one action in the blame mode might be to seek revenge on the perpetrator.'

It's not fair that he's free and I'm ruined for life. I swear, I'll get back at him somehow.

'Another channel for your anger might be to join organised groups which encourage female power. In this way you form a common bond with other women who likewise tend to view men as contemptible and women as more worthy of your time and emotional investment.'

Tessa nodded her understanding.

Reaction pattern 3: healthiness

Finally, I uncovered the bottom part of the chart.

'The third kind of reaction is what God would really have us do, Tessa. That is both to acknowledge the damage, and to seek healing and forgiveness. This is the cognitive response. You would recognise the emotions and confusion, but yield them to God's Holy Spirit.'

I don't understand all this, Lord. Please help me understand what I'm feeling and work it through.

'And you would pursue a course of healthy actions in line with what God would endorse.'

I'll locate a good counsellor or support group. I'll educate myself by attending seminars and reading books on this issue. I'll be vulnerable as I know how to be for now, share my situation with a few other Christians and receive prayer. I'll determine to continue relating with men, even though a man hurt me. What-

ever it takes to give God permission and tools to use in my life for healing, I'll try to do it.

I stopped again so Tessa could absorb everything.

After a while she responded. 'It all seems so hard, Jeanette.'

'Yes, it does,' I nodded. Then I made sure we had eye contact before making my next statement. 'But the very fact that you're here, wanting to deal with the roots of your lesbianism, means you're on the right track already, Tessa. That's what is important right now. The denial and blame patterns are types of slavery that bring misery. In my own life, the fear of pain prevented me from leaving the denial position for a long time. Until I was willing to walk out of that way of life, I was unable to go any further in my healing. But you're taking the healthy approach. That means you want real freedom to go on with life to its fullest. And I know from Scripture, my own experience, and other ex-lesbians' experiences that God will honour the healthiness perspective.'

Her eyes were filling with tears, but Tessa managed to smile.

Trunk = attitudes and fruit = by-products

I pointed at the next picture in the series of roots diagrams. 'Let's move on to Diagram 3, which shows the tree. Once your seed is planted in the soil and begins to grow, a shoot sprouts up, breaking through the surface. As it grows over time, the shoot is strengthened and becomes the trunk of the tree. The trunk carries nutrients and poisons from the soil up to the leaves and fruit.'

Tessa thought for a moment, then summarised the analogy. 'So this trunk represents my attitudes which have grown from my original root reactions to the soil.'

'Exactly! And many different attitudes or strategies can result from similar soils in which people are planted.'

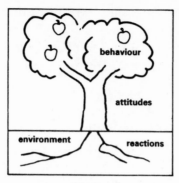

Diagram 3

'Could you give me some examples?' Tessa queried.

'Well, one woman might use subtle manipulation to cope, while another tries helpless submission. You know, the doormat type that everyone can walk all over.'

That caught her attention. 'Yes.' Tessa leaned forward, 'I've seen plenty of those two kinds.'

I agreed. 'There are other types of attitudes common in both the lesbian and the straight world. Some women might use untrusting self-sufficiency as a strategy. Someone else could turn to needy over-dependence on others. All these different trunk attitudes come from your cognitive assessment of life, and your emotional response to it. The trunk nourishes a variety of fruit, which grow as a by-product of your attitudes.'

'This is a good illustration, Jeanette. I think I'm really getting this,' Tessa said.

'Good. Then let's go all the way through an example. Suppose your attitude is: *I'm not worth anything; I am unloved and unlovable.* Then one fruit in your life appears as low self-esteem.

'Strange as it seems, often we act out low self-esteem in pridefulness. *I feel like I'm nothing, but I'm going to hide it from everyone. They wouldn't like me if they really knew me, so*

I won't give them the chance. So my pride has leaped into action, because I will prove to people that I have worth, even though underneath I don't believe it myself. Though it may masquerade as something else, it is still self-centredness.'

Trying to pick off the fruit

That seemed to spark some frustration for Tessa. 'That's all very well, Jeanette,' she said, brow furrowed. 'But what do I do? How do I fix my low self-esteem? I could try to take the fruit off the tree, but that's not going to change anything if more keeps growing back!'

'You're right. We've got to get down to the root of things. We can't change the soil. We can't change the environment or the offenses that have come along during our lives. But we can do something about our root reactions by offering them to Jesus and asking him to change them. And as he changes our reactions, over time, that will change our attitudes and strategies. And then the fruit will change.

'Fruit are only symptoms of deeper issues. If I just took the fruit off my tree, I still have the same roots feeding from the same soil. I'll just produce another crop of similar fruit, or perhaps switch to another type of fruit that is an equally destructive attempt to meet my own needs.

'I could chop the tree down, but I'm still left with the roots. The roots are alive and receiving nutrition—even if it is poor nutrition—from the soil. Roots are resilient. Some form of tree and fruit will regrow from them. So, to change the fruit, I need to let Jesus deal with the bad roots, so the good roots can flourish. Because not all roots are bad!'

Tessa fidgeted, then crossed her arms, pouting. Her unruly blond hair briefly veiled her penetrating stare.

'So—an example from lesbianism. That's what I want, Jeanette,' she demanded, obviously frustrated.

'Think of homosexual behaviour as the fruit on the tree. Say you stop going to bed with women. That in itself won't satisfy your legitimate need for intimacy with women—to give and receive love, to be nurtured and feel secure. Eventually you are tempted to return to old methods of trying to meet those needs. Sadly, more often than not, it's merely a question of time before a new crop of fruit—homosexual acting out—grows again. Maybe even a bumper crop!

'I've known women who've abstained from sex for twelve or thirteen years. When they're overwhelmed with their neediness and the wrong situation comes along, they fall back into sin because they haven't dealt with root issues.'

Tessa uncrossed her arms and leaned forward.

I continued. 'So you have a choice here, Tessa. You can pick the fruit off the tree by trying to change behaviours. Or you can chop the tree down by trying to change attitudes over a period of time. Or you can go to the source—the roots. You can change the whole tree from being a weak, disease-rooted tree into a fine oak—strong and sturdy—by dealing with the roots.'

'It's not fair!' Tessa blurted out, her fists clenched. 'I've tried digging up the bad roots, but I just can't change.'

The root of Jesse is the tree of life

'That's exactly the point. We can't change ourselves. That's where Jesus comes in, Tessa. Jesus is the only one who can deal effectively with our roots.'

The truth seemed to be sinking in. Tessa calmed herself down, then simply asked, 'How?'

I put down all my charts and diagrams. 'First, let's review the wrong way—when we try to deal with the roots ourselves. I think most of us dealing with lesbianism believe at some point that we can correct everything ourselves. Often God just lets us give that approach our best shot. Usually we end up totally frustrated with working life out on our own.'

Tessa sighed. 'That's where I've been lately. That's why I came in today, asking for answers.'

'Then you're reading for God's grace. When we finally get tired of gritting our teeth and white-knuckling our way through life, God is there, eagerly waiting to take over. But he's a gentleman and doesn't force his plan on us.'

I could see some relief in Tessa's eyes. 'Tell me again how Jesus fits into all of this, Jeanette.'

'The events in your past, your soil, don't change. But the Lord can change the painful feelings you associate with memories of past hurts.'

Tessa's eyes got wide. 'Is that what healing prayer is all about?'

'Yes,' I answered. 'Suppose you think back to some particular hurtful incident from when you were a child. The memory fills you with incredible pain and a sense of loss. As you ask Jesus to enter that memory, you recognise that he was with you all of the time. In fact, he is able to walk with you through your pain, leaving healed places where raw, open wounds used to be.'

'You mean that Jesus is there but doesn't do anything to stop the problem?' Tessa seemed shocked.

'Yes.'

Tessa's eyes blazed with fury. 'I'd be so angry with him, just standing there and watching me hurt. If he cares so much, why doesn't he do something?'

I paused, not wanting to give some pat answer. Yet the answer is simple, though not necessarily easy to accept. 'It boils down to free will, Tessa. The ability to choose is something God granted every one of us from the beginning. We have a choice either to follow God, or to do our own thing. If we are bent on sinning, then God will not violate that choice. He will grieve at the harm we do to ourselves and those around us, but he will not intervene.'

Tessa sat silent, her eyes remained focused on the carpet.

I continued. 'Anger is part of the healing process, Tessa. It's okay to feel angry. What we do with that anger will prove helpful or detrimental to our healing. We can use it for destruction or as a springboard to dealing with our issues.'

Tessa shifted in her chair as I continued my brief explanation of healing prayer. 'It may take many times of working through that particular event before there is substantial healing, but healing can come. Your memory of the event won't disappear, but your reaction to it will. Then, over time, Jesus alters your attitudes. You will begin to see life from his perspective. It's like getting a new pair of eyes—like Amy Grant sings about in *My Father's Eyes*! Having God's perspective.'

Tessa perked up. 'Wow! I always liked that song, and what you just said puts it into a whole new light for me. I'll still have to work through the free will issue, though. It just seems so unfair.'

Nourished by the Living Water—Jesus

I smiled, because I understood her position from my own experience. 'Give yourself some time on that. Meanwhile, let's go on with the good news. Your new thoughts and attitudes eventually effect changes in your actions. It's a process, Tessa, but the Lord can touch the roots and pour out his healing balm on the pain you feel.'

I asked Tessa to turn in her Bible to Ezekiel 47:12 and read it aloud. 'Fruit trees of all kinds will grow on both sides of the river. Their leaves will not wither, nor will their fruit fail. Every month they will bear, because the water from the sanctuary flows to them. Their fruit will serve for food and their leaves for healing.'

After she finished reading the passage, I noticed her eyes had filled with tears again. I handed her a tissue and continued. 'Once we allow Jesus to enter our pain, Tess, it's like he grafts us into his root system. And he fertilises our soil with Living Water so our tree can flourish. So we aren't destined to feed from poor soil for the rest of our lives.'

Hope seemed to be springing back up for Tessa. 'So where do I begin?' she exclaimed. 'It seems such an enormous task!'

'Well, let's be realistic—it is hard, but the Lord can handle it. We're not going to go digging. We need to let the Lord tackle all the bad roots. He has a perfect order for dealing with them, and his order for you may not be the same as for me. He doesn't treat us as a forest! He treats us as individual trees.'

Suddenly Tessa looked at her watch. 'I can't believe it! That hour went so fast, considering the stuff we covered was pretty heavy!'

I smiled. 'You are definitely going to need some time to think through all of this! Take a copy of my diagrams and let the Holy Spirit guide you through them on your own.'

I also handed Tessa a sheet of questions. Startled, she looked at me wide-eyed. 'Homework!'

She turned her head and shot me a side-long, impish glance, then read the list aloud.

1. Ask God to show you which root issues he wants to work on with you now.

2. What do you feel are some of your faulty attitudes that keep you from bearing good fruit?

3. What personal application can you make from the parable of the sower in Matthew 13?

4. Can you identify your typical 'reaction pattern'? Ask Jesus to guide you through 'healing'.

5. What are some of the fruit you are bearing that you would like to have changed?

Tessa peeked at me over the top of the paper. 'When do you want this done, teacher, by tomorrow?'

I laughed. 'I think it's time to pray!'

After prayer, Tessa left and I considered our next step. I knew that her relationship with her mother was troubling Tessa, and sensed the Lord's leading to approach that root area first.

For your information

The title, Root of Jesse, is another name for Jesus Christ. Jesse was the father of King David, of Old Testament fame. The genealogies of Jesus in Matthew 1 and Luke 3 both list Jesse as a forefather of Jesus. The main scriptural reference to the Root of Jesse comes in Isaiah 11:10: 'In that day the nations shall seek after the root of Jesse, who shall stand as a banner for the peoples, and his resting place shall be glorious' (Modern Language Bible).

For further study

1. *A Door of Hope* by Jan Frank (Here's Life Publishers: USA, 1987).
2. *The Wounded Heart: Hope for Adult Victims of Childhood Sexual Abuse* by Dr Dan B Allender (NavPress: USA, 1990).
3. *Pain and Pretending: You can be set free from the hurts of the past* by Rich Buhler (Thomas Nelson: USA, 1988).
4. *Healing for Damaged Emotions* by David A Seamands (Victor Books: USA, 1981) (UK edition: Scripture Press, 1986).
5. *Healing of Memories* by David A Seamands (Victor Books: USA, 1985) (UK edition: Scripture Press, 1986).

CHAPTER FIVE

MOTHERS AND DAUGHTERS: FOUR STORIES

I didn't have to be in ex-gay ministry for long before I discovered that the whole 'mother issue' loomed up in almost every conversation I had with women. These discussions about mums raised a variety of reactions from the different women, depending on their experience. In this chapter we will hear from four women: Eleanor, Cindy, Louise and Alison.

Each had a different style of mother/daughter relationship, though several had similar types of mothers. As each shares her story, it is likely that confusing or painful feelings will surface. Perhaps you'll feel intense heaviness and sorrow. Perhaps sharp pain or anger. Perhaps nothing at all. Those are all okay. Take a moment to give God permission to allow whatever feelings to surface which he may want to heal in you.

The dispassionate mother: Eleanor's story

Neither cold nor hot, Eleanor's mother was lukewarm toward her daughter, as if in rebellion to the scriptural principle, 'Can a mother forget her child?' (see Isaiah 49:15).

While growing up, Eleanor's apparent indifference toward her mother thinly veiled unexpressed anger Eleanor had at their shallow relationship. Instead of developing a close mother/daughter relationship, they behaved more like two boxers, skirting around the ring, sizing each other up. Neither party had any intention of ever throwing a punch and connecting.

I detected a sense of isolation from my mother at a very young age. I don't remember any particular event which fostered this emotional distance. It was more of an inability to communicate honestly with each other that furthered the sense of separation I was experiencing. As I grew up, I remember spending much of my time observing my mother rather than connecting with her emotionally. I knew that I was meant to feel something about this woman who washed and ironed my clothes, fed me and gave me spending money. But I did not. Sometimes I would try to muster up a feeling. But I could not. Emotionally, I was numb.

And yet there was some unexplained need for connection between us. Even after I had grown up and left home physically, I knew that I had not left emotionally. The physical distance between us now accented emotions I had been feeling, but previously felt unable to identify.

Mum and I had this agreement that she would call me every Tuesday night at seven o'clock sharp. I looked forward to her call, anticipating our exchange of thoughts, feelings and desires. But it never happened. As soon as I heard her voice on the other end of the phone, I would freeze. I wanted to say things like, 'I love you.' But the words would stick in my throat.

So we would chit-chat. It was the same script every week—only it wasn't funny. She would tell me about the dog, the neighbours, what she had seen on television—and my dad. The order was always the same. She never asked me about me. The conversation was strictly one way. I suppose I didn't volunteer the information either. I did try once or twice, but she acted like she didn't hear me. It was as though part of me, anything below the surface, didn't exist.

After she'd hang up, I would get angry. I couldn't understand why we never had a 'real' conversation. It always appeared that we just talked *at* each other, instead of *with* each other. Without fail I would vow that I would not let it affect me. I would just get on with my life and pretend the call never happened.

Then Tuesday would loom up again. And I would go through the same routine. *Tonight will be different*, I'd hope. *Tonight will be real.* But it never was.

I wanted my feelings about mum and our relationship to change. I knew that as a Christian I had the opportunity to implement change. But I felt helpless and fearful. I became fearful of losing our flimsy relationship. *If I start making waves, will I lose everything?* At least this Tuesday night routine was predictable. It wasn't much of a relationship, but it was better than nothing.

Along with the fear, I felt as though I was swinging on some emotional pendulum. My early days of indifference had long since been replaced with emotional turbulence. Some days I would love my mother with unbridled passion, other days I would hate her with equal intensity. Some days I didn't know what I really wanted! From her—or myself. Confusion reigned.

Why do I need this relationship now? That question confused me the most. The indifference I had seemingly felt as a child had gradually been replaced by a growing need to emotionally connect with her.

I thought that when I became a Christian those yearnings would disappear. I became quite adept at suppressing my needs for nurture, love, acceptance and affirmation. After all, God promised to meet all of my needs, and if I still had these emotional needs, then I wasn't much of a Christian.

Now I realise how my understanding was confused. I had hurts that required healing before I would be able to receive all the nurture, love and security that God was offering me. I had to learn how to let down my defensive walls of self-sufficiency, control and pride in order to let Jesus in. That was frightening! I had to make a major decision. Did I want to *look* healthy, or *be* healthy? I chose the latter.

How did my decision to let God in affect my relationship with my mother? Well, I realised that I had to establish some boundaries in my life and also take some initiative in the relationship. The next step I took was to make a list of all that I wanted to say to Mum, and then I would call *her*. Since I was making the call, that would allow me the freedom to say what I wanted, and express my own feelings instead of waiting for her to acknowledge them.

By five pm the next Tuesday, I had made my list. I decided it was time to tell her the names of those I lived with, and describe my house and neighbourhood. I wanted to explain my job more fully, and how satisfied I was with it. I wanted to tell her how important my Christianity was to me. And I was going to tell her how I felt now that my best friend had moved out of town.

The first conversation I initiated was not an astounding success. But I did manage to say one item on my list. I realised that my initial expectations were too high. But I felt good about myself for letting God give me the courage to phone her.

My relationship with my mother is still far from ideal. She still doesn't know my true feelings toward her. But I'm listening to God more now than I used to. I know that he will continue to guide me through this process with Mum.

The manipulative mother: Cindy's story

Cindy's anger remained hidden until after the death of her mother. But she had condemned her mother and acted upon those judgements long before that point. The relationship was based on mutual distrust, which prevented a close bond from ever taking place.

One afternoon, when I was four years old, my grandfather teased me incessantly and hurt my feelings. This caused me to cry. My father, not knowing how to respond, took me to a bedroom and told me to stay there until I could pull myself together.

I felt confused and hurt. I sensed that I was being punished for doing something bad. My mother supported Dad's action one hundred per cent. She said nothing to me when I came back downstairs. She just nodded her approval of my complying with dad's directive.

That was typical of Mum's reactions. She didn't protect me from dad and his verbal insensitivity toward me. She preferred to warn me and give me manipulative ways to act that would be pleasing to him. From that teasing incident onward, I started protecting my feelings. I vowed not to share the emotional side of myself with my mum or dad again. That decision obviously created walls between us. Thus began the long journey of mutual distrust between me and them.

During my early teenage years this distrust took its toll. I developed a mindset regarding my mum that went something like this: *She doesn't have a mind of her own. She is completely afraid of Dad and under his thumb. She would prefer to lie to him and manipulate him rather than to face confrontation.* Some of this was true. Dad would leave for days if a verbal fight with Mum heated up too much. I'm sure Mum was afraid that he would never come back.

There was little honest communication or integrity with my parents and me. I just lived several lives. One at home that was resentfully compliant. One at school that was an overachiever. One on my personal time that kept trying to find meaning, love and acceptance. Eventually I turned to hiding my feelings and numbing them through alcohol to even cope with the world.

Then, in my third year of college, I met a woman who seemed to give me unconditional love. This was just what I'd been seeking for years. Before long the relationship became physical. We lived together almost five years.

I never told mum about my homosexual involvement, and never suspected she knew my secret. But a few years ago, I was talking with my sister about our growing up. She said that mum once told her to beware of me because I was living with my flatmate 'like a man lives with a woman'. I was stunned by this revelation.

My mother died several years after I became a Christian. Although I had left the lesbian lifestyle, I had never worked through any 'mother issues'. Instead, I was too busy figuring out how to live as a Christian. At the time of her death, I was still blaming my father—not my mother—for the outcome of my life's choices. The initial resolution of 'mother issues' came years later.

After my mum's death, I mentally and emotionally enshrined her. No longer could I blame her for any of my problems. Whatever she had done was now a closed book. I reasoned it would be wrong to blame the dead. After all, she could no longer defend herself.

Several years after Mum died, I submitted myself to Christian psychotherapy. During that process I realised how I'd put mum on a pedestal. I relayed to my counsellor a picture of a perfect mother, and described our relationship as perfect, but distant. When my counsellor confronted me with that, I realised that I'd been fooling myself. I began the long process of taking an honest look at my relationship with Mum.

Eventually, my repressed emotions surfaced, and I was

able to express anger. I was angry at Mum with regard to Dad. I resented her protection of him at my expense. I distinctly remembered her lying to me to avoid confrontation with Dad. Somehow, I felt that I had been the recipient of her brokenness, that she had passed it on to me. I saw her extreme dependence, masked by a false front of manipulation, and I also resented her invalidation of my emotions in order to 'keep the peace'. Her worst fear was losing Dad and she went to any length to keep him from leaving.

Since I felt I couldn't yell at a dead woman, I drove into the countryside, mumbling and grumbling all the way. On returning home, I beat my pillow against my bed, yelling out in anger and frustration.

A turning point came when I began to get in touch with my mum's own brokenness and family dysfunction. This new perspective helped me begin to understand why she did some of the things she did. That gave me a sense of compassion for her. I sought prayer for the ability to forgive her and to bring healing to my mum's and my relationship.

During the prayer time with a female prayer counsellor, I imagined my mum sitting in the living room. Although very ill, she motioned for me to come and sit with her. She just wanted me to be close, to put her hand on mine. She said, 'I love you, Dear.' And I responded with, 'I love you, Mum.'

After some time of just relishing that moment, I knew that it was time to tell her all those hidden things that I had been too scared to reveal. I told her the good news first. Although I had been in a lesbian relationship, I was now out. From her reaction I could see that she had known this for some time. I shared that I was so changed by Christ that there would never be another woman in my life in that way. She said she knew and that she was proud of me. She affirmed that she would love me either way that I chose to go, but that she was glad that I had made a change.

Encouraged, I told her that she had hurt me and I told her of several memories of feeling betrayed or abandoned. She responded with, 'Darling, I'm so sorry. Please forgive me.' We both cried. I put my head on her chest and just let the tears roll. (In actuality I had wrapped my arms around the woman with whom I was praying.)

After a time the tears slowed down and I told her that I was aware of not giving her many chances for reconciliation. I had rejected her early in my life and I asked her to forgive me. More tears and hugging followed.

At the end of this encounter Mum told me that she had to go now and that I had to let go of her. I didn't want to, but I said, 'Okay.'

After the prayer time was over, I realised that I had soaked an entire box of tissues with my tears. I had a feeling for the first time that Jesus was in control of the relationship with Mum. No longer was anger at Mum controlling me. It was as though I'd handed her over to Jesus. At the same time he was very present with me, comforting me. There was a sense of closure between my mum and me that had never been there before.

The 'my-best-friend' mother: Louise's story

Louise, my room-mate at a conference, made a shocking statement: 'You know, Jeanette, I realise now that I was my mum's best friend.' This came as a complete surprise—I'd never heard of such a thing! Yet, since I began working in ministry to ex-lesbians several years ago, I have encountered a small number of other women who were best friends with their mothers.

Louise's relationship with her mother made for one major problem. Louise became an 'enabler' to her mother in the midst of their friendship—she let her mother's own needs control the relationship. In many respects she protected and parented the very one who should have protected and parented her. This role reversal prohibited emotional growth in either Louise or her mother.

I used to attend small group meetings, but I found it really difficult to relate to all the women who seemed to connect all negative feelings to their mothers. I felt their attitude was too simplistic and basically unfair.

They would laugh at me when I said I had no 'mother issues'. But I meant it. How could I? Mum and I were best friends.

People used to treat us as sisters. There wasn't anything that she wouldn't share with me. I first became her confidante when she and dad split up. She would creep into my bedroom at night, and pour out her heart to me. I don't know how much help a ten-year-old girl can be at a time like that, but it felt good to be able to help my mother in some way. She needed me and I was glad to have those special times with her.

That's why I was confused as to my lesbian involvement. I didn't fit into the 'classic' mould of 'negative' mother/daughter relationships.

So, I asked God if my special friendship with mum had any bearing on my lesbianism, and if so, to bring healing. God is faithful. He showed me my 'mother issue' by leading me to make a list of my past lovers. It wasn't until then that I realised a startling fact. All five of them were at least fifteen years my senior. They all belonged to my mother's generation!

A week after making that list, I remembered praying one night. While praying, God reminded me of an incident that happened when I was eleven.

My friends arrived at the house to take me roller skating. As I kissed my mother 'goodbye' she leaned back on the sofa and moaned softly. 'Don't go, dear,' she whispered. 'Mummy needs you here.'

I glanced at my friends, who were impatiently waiting by the front door. 'But, Mum,' I began, trying to loosen her grip of my arm. It was no good. She looked at me with those mournful eyes and I knew there would be no roller skating that afternoon.

Before that memory had settled, God reminded me of other incidents from my childhood: the birthday party I had to excuse myself from; the disappointment at missing summer camp; the cocktail party I had to attend as a twelve-year-old; and comforting Mum several times when I found her sobbing in the bathroom.

I noticed a knot forming in my stomach as these memories flooded back to me. I clenched my fists involuntarily, and my body became rigid.

For the first time in my life I felt anger toward my mother. *My childhood disappeared with her divorce. I lost all my friends because of her. Where was she when I needed her? I wanted a mother, not a friend!*

Sixteen years of anger and hurt surfaced that night as I realised the truth of my situation. I sobbed for the child who suddenly had to grow up. I wept for the twelve-year-old whose friends left her one by one until she was without playmates.

Through further counselling I understood how I'd missed out on the nurturing and sense of protection I should have received from my mum. Not only had I missed out, but I had also taken on the role of nurturer and protector of my mother when my parents divorced.

I didn't need long to tie the loose ends together regarding my past lovers. Not only were their ages similar, but I also looked to them to provide care and security in my life. I certainly accepted a 'childlike' role in our relationships. I was probably trying to recapture those missing years.

Fortunately, I was able to communicate this sense of

loss to my mother. She was so ashamed at first, but God really helped her deal with it. I forgave her for placing me in the role of caretaker. I asked her to forgive me for not allowing her to move out of that role of 'child'.

There was a time of grieving over the past together and what should have been. But through honest communication, we were eventually able to build a new, solid relationship which has become a delight to both of us.

The self-consumed mother: Alison's story

Many women have entered the motherhood role too young physically and/or emotionally, or otherwise are very needy. Therefore they are incapable of nurturing their children as they should—they still need to be nurtured themselves.

Alison grew up with expectations that her mother, an alcoholic, did not meet. By later closing the door to anything her mum may have offered, Alison blocked further bonding between the two.

While I drove home after an intense inner healing seminar, I recalled a statement Leanne Payne had made. 'If you're having trouble seeing pictures of childhood events that you've asked Jesus to reveal to you for the purpose of healing, sometimes it's due to deep-rooted sorrow. The initial cause of that sorrow must be dealt with before healing can continue.'

During the seminar, I never could see any pictures of my childhood. I had thought my pride wouldn't allow them to surface, but now I wondered if it really was because of sorrow. I pulled the car over and turned off the engine. I breathed deeply and spoke aloud. 'Lord, I don't want to be weighed down with such sorrow. I can't believe that I am, but you must be leading this, so please help me to understand.'

Immediately, I experienced a deep sorrow about my relationship with my father. Although I thought I'd forgiven him completely, many specific, unhealed incidents came to mind. I repented of my unforgiveness toward him. I asked the Lord to heal my old responses to past hurts. In my spirit I sensed only a bit of relief. *There must be more to come*, I thought.

I began the same process with my mother. To my surprise, the pain and sorrow went much deeper. I wanted to resist and return to safety, but resolved to press on. The more things that I spoke out in forgiveness toward Mum (and myself), the harder I cried until I was wailing. I begged God to help me regain control of my emotions. But long-buried feelings had erupted, and there was no hope of immediate control being regained.

Through tears, I continued. 'I forgive you, Mum, for not being the mother I wanted you to be. I forgive you that alcohol consumed your life and you weren't able to see much beyond that. I forgive you for... for never holding me in love.'

I was startled at the words that had just come out of my mouth. I sat silently while the reality sank in. Then came more tears. *That's it, isn't it, Jesus? That's why I'm grieving. My mother never held me.*

No, she'd never nurtured me—at least, that's the way *I'd* seen it. Now it made sense! That's why I eventually turned to lesbianism. I was always looking to other women to satisfy my need for my mother's love.

A new reality struck me. I had withdrawn from any affection Mum may actually have tried to show me because I feared subsequent rejection. She may have tried, but I wouldn't receive because I was in rebellion. *No wonder lesbianism was a frustratingly hopeless lifestyle,* I thought. *It was built on rejection and rebellion.*

I sat in silence while the Lord wrapped my soul with comfort, peace and love. What a release I felt! *I've carried this weight of sorrow so long that it just felt natural*. Delight overcame me as I *truly* forgave my mother for her lack of affection and forgave myself for withdrawing from her and blocking any subsequent attempts at nurturing me.

'This is just the beginning, Alison,' the Lord seemed to be saying. At last I understood the root causes of my strained relationship with Mum. And I knew he would lead me to whatever I needed to do next to set things right. The answer was simply, 'Pray.' God knew that I couldn't just run and tell her everything that had happened that day—she wouldn't understand. So I prayed and asked him to set up the right opportunities to begin healing the relationship.

The next few times I saw Mum after the inner healing experience, I noticed that I was feeling differently toward her. I could sense the birthing of a renewal in our relationship, but nothing exceptional was occurring. Each time I went to visit, I prayed that the Lord would use me to express his love in whatever way he decided. Also, I asked for his help in removing any barriers I might be imposing and for any expectations I might be placing on Mum.

About a month later after the experience, I received a phone call. Mum and dad invited me over to watch *Jesus of Nazareth* on TV. They teased me, saying that I could help interpret the story, but added that it would be nice to have the family together at Easter. I agreed.

We all sat quietly, waiting for the final segment of the film. Jesus was about to die on the cross. Then, without any cue from me, my mother looked at me and said, 'Alison, why don't you come over here and sit next to me?' I could hardly believe my ears! After sitting a moment in astonishment, I seized the opportunity. I curled up on the sofa, with my head on her lap as a child would, and my mummy stroked my hair with loving, gentle caresses as we watched Jesus, the Healer, being crucified.

I looked up at her and said, 'We haven't done this in a long time,' although in my mind I thought, *We've never done this.*

'I know,' she whispered. 'This feels so good. We'll have to do it more often.'

I was content. Tears began to flow slowly as I marvelled at the goodness of my Lord. I turned back toward the television set and watched the part where Jesus dies. What an appropriate moment to experience the birth of the love relationship God intended for a mother and daughter to share.

Mum looked at me. 'Are you crying that Christ is being crucified?'

'Yes,' I answered. 'And I love you, Mum.'

She gently smiled. 'I love you, too.'

CHAPTER SIX

MOTHERS AND DAUGHTERS: DIGGING DEEPER

There is a temptation to oversimplify the problem of the mother/daughter relationship in order to clarify the situation and move toward a solution. But oversimplification would do injustice to both parties involved. Lesbianism is not a one-two-three problem with an equally simple solution. If it were, we would see many more healed women in a comparatively shorter time than is presently the case. So, in sharing some insights on mother/daughter relationships, I will do my best to avoid a cut-and-dried, black-and-white mentality.

The reparative drive

Dr Elizabeth Moberly, a research psychologist, has arrived at some interesting and helpful conclusions from her study of homosexuals. I encourage you to read her book, *Homosexuality: A New Christian Ethic*, listed at the end of the chapter.

Dr Moberly makes it clear that our needs for security, love, and affirmation from members of the same sex are legitimate needs. They should have been secured in the daughter through the nurturing and bonding between herself and her mother.

For some reason, the daughter sees her mother as not being benevolent, involved, and concerned about the daughter's needs. This may be based on real or perceived actions by the mother. In either case, this breakdown in that emotional bonding process between mother and daughter creates a same-sex love deficit in the daughter. Although this deficit is real and requires attention, the daughter copes through unconscious methods of correcting the damage. This urge to repair the damage is called the 'reparative drive'.

At first, the daughter may notice a deep longing to 'connect' with her mother—receive her love and attention. At puberty, this longing becomes sexualised. Seeking out lesbian relationships, therefore, can be seen as an unconscious attempt to restore what was missing in the crucial relationship between the mother and daughter.

When we become consciously aware of our sinful attempts to gain security, love, and affirmation, we can refocus on godly methods—such as healthy same-sex friendships. We will explore this topic in chapter 10.

'Categorising' mothers

It would be nice to lay out a neat set of categories to describe different mothers. However, no mother falls exclusively into one particular category to the exclusion of others. But in speaking with various ex-lesbian women, I do see certain patterns developing about their mothers. I will address these general patterns.

The first 'type' of mother adopts the 'doormat' mentality. Although she may be kind, sincere, and ever-giving, the lesbian struggler perceives her as downtrodden, weak and ineffective. The daughter has little or no respect for her, and sees her mother as subject to the whims of men and of society in general.

The second 'type' of mother comes across as domineering, dogmatic and determined not to let a man get in the way of what she wants. Sometimes her life situation has encouraged these attitudes. Perhaps the husband is an alcoholic and has abdicated responsibility. The wife not only has to manage the house and family, but often becomes the major 'breadwinner'. She may be a single mother who has had an uphill struggle from the onset, and has had to fight her way through life in order to survive.

The third 'type' of mother is often seen as a conniving and critical manipulator. The mother may not have learned how to express her desires in an open, honest way. Therefore, she resorts to quiet manipulation to get what she wants. She has a tendency to be critical of everybody, although rarely to their faces. Without the mother expressing honesty and openness, the daughter is unable to form a relationship based on trust, but is troubled by thoughts: *How do I know what she is saying is true? What is she saying to others about me?* The daughter reacts to these fears by withdrawing from the mother.

Many mothers do not fall into any of the above descriptions. However, the daughter who struggles with lesbianism feels misunderstood by her mother. Often there are no specific incidents a daughter can point to, but the sense of separation is real and evidenced in their present interactions.

We need only look at the four women mentioned in chapter 5 to see the variety of dynamics in mother/daughter relationships. Like those four women, how often have we set our own agenda for our lives, held tight to it and refused to receive anything else that may be offered? Sometimes we need to stand back and take an objective look at our life situations to see how we have truncated our personal growth, and that of those around us.

Mum's own problems

Another striking similarity appears to be common among the mothers of lesbians. A large number of mothers, in the estimation of their daughters, do not feel completely secure in their role as a woman or as a mother and caregiver.

If this is true, what relevance does the mother's own insecure feminine identity have on the daughter's maturation process?

It is my belief that this denial, or inability to accept her own sexuality, results in anxiety for the mother. This anxiety may cause the mother to react negatively to her daughter's own emerging sexuality. The daughter, in turn, draws from her mother's anxiety. At the very least, the child may deduce that it is difficult to be a woman. This problem can deepen, depending on the messages the daughter receives from her father or other significant males. Their inability or unwillingness to affirm her femininity and worth may steer her towards a life-changing conclusion—it is not okay to be a woman.

If a mother is unable to make her daughter feel appreciated and acceptable as a woman, the girl will have difficulty integrating herself with the rest of the female world. If the emerging adolescent is ever to feel good about herself, she needs to identify with a positive female role model.

For many of us, the only role model we encountered was our mother. Healthy development was usually thwarted because we perceived our mother—our main role model—as sexless, unaffirming and/or inadequate.

Sometimes it takes another person to stir our memories or clarify our attitudes regarding our mums. I recently spoke to Carol concerning my speculations about mother issues.

Carol's conclusions

'Carol,' I asked, 'can you relate to what I am saying?'

'You know, I was thinking only recently that my mother wasn't quite normal,' she mused. 'She wasn't gay or anything like that. But when I was young I would notice how she'd look at my aunts. Their clothes and hair were always in fashion. I would catch my mother just looking at them. I don't think she was envious, but you could tell she didn't really think she fitted in. My aunts enjoyed each other's company. My mother would sit, almost motionless. She'd be in the group, but she wouldn't talk. She'd smile, but I could tell that she wasn't truly there with them. She felt uncomfortable. I never felt she liked herself as a woman. I don't think she was really happy.'

Having met her mother, I was surprised. 'But your mum looked great when I saw her. What happened?'

'My older sister, Beth, went to college. That Christmas, after the first term, she returned home clutching a large bag of make-up. My mother and I exchanged furtive glances as Beth set up the "salon".

'I lost interest as soon as Beth told me that I couldn't use soap on my face. But my mother persevered. For the rest of the vacation they were like a couple of teenagers, "experimenting" with colours and styles.'

I was intrigued. 'And then?' I urged.

'After Beth returned to college, Mum bought make-up and really started looking after herself. She had a new zest for life. What I really found amazing was the change in dynamics when my aunts visited. Mum was self-conscious at first, but they accepted and encouraged her. They were amazed at the transformation. It wasn't long before she was conversing and laughing with her sisters.'

Carol paused. 'I guess that separated us even more. I couldn't relate to her new-found femininity. When I saw the interaction between Mum and my sister, I realised what was missing between Mum and me.'

Carol laughed ironically. 'You see, they have a relationship. Mum listens to her. It's not without its problems, but they've got something going. I guess that's what I'd really like.'

Although I didn't believe that this incident was the beginning of her estrangement from her mother, I sensed this episode in Carol's life reinforced her detachment.

Detachment

It is important to recognise that whatever the reason behind the mother's attitude and behaviour, the daughter grows up forming her own opinions of what she does and does not want. Consciously and/or unconsciously, the daughter embraces some of her mother's ideas and characteristics and rejects others. The little girl makes some important, life-changing decisions about identity based on the input she receives. Some girls make these major decisions early in adolescence. More often, girls make monumental decisions (conscious or subconscious) about their identity at a much earlier age.

A breakdown in relationships may occur from seemingly minor events such as Carol's, to heartbreaking episodes involving physical abuse. Unless this deterioration is stopped, the child progressively detaches herself from the tenuous mother/daughter bond.

This detachment from Mum constitutes one major root of lesbianism. But, again, we must keep in mind that the network of roots is complex. Other major roots include the father/daughter relationship, dysfunctional family issues, peer influence, and trauma. Just because two women have similar backgrounds in all these areas, that does not mean both will necessarily become lesbians.

Healing the mother/daughter relationship

Perhaps this whole area of mothers stirs up feelings within you. Relax. You do not have to reach a solution today. However, I do know that the broken relationship with your mother, unless resolved, really prevents a clean break from lesbianism.

There is no 'zap' method of bridging this rift between mother and daughter. It took a number of years to develop, and it will take time to mend. If you give yourself time to work out the relationship with your mother, change will happen—at least in *your* life.

It is possible that your mum may not want healing in your relationship, or does not have the emotional capability to re-bond with you. Despite your legitimate sadness at this problem, God can still help you consciously work through the situation and find healing in your own heart. God can be as a mother to you. 'Although my father and my mother have forsaken me, yet the Lord will take me up [adopt me as His child] (Ps 27:10, AMPLIFIED).

Regardless of how your mother/daughter relationship goes, the Lord will help you address a number of important areas as your journey out of lesbianism progresses. Think of these new attitudes and actions as new shoots and fruits springing from roots that Jesus is healing. The lists of issues and methods I suggest in this chapter are not exhaustive. It is my desire to point you in the right direction. There are many good books listed at the end of the chapter, which will bring greater understanding to any specific area.

Awareness

We cannot begin to deal with an issue until we know that there is a problem! Often, denial prevents us from entering into greater healing. Denial is failure or refusal to acknowledge the reality that a problem exists.

For example, it took Susan a long time to acknowledge that she was angry with her mother. Even admitting that she had almost thrust a carving knife in her mum's back did not break through the denial. When Susan's counsellor questioned her about anger towards her mother, Susan vehemently refuted holding such an emotion. 'I was disappointed in her,' was all the explanation she would volunteer.

Was Susan trying to mislead the counsellor? I believe not. Five years after the incident, Susan began to experience feelings of anger. At first it was without focus, a kind of 'free-floating' anger. But, with prayerful counsel and a desire for healing, Susan was able to discern that the core of her anger was toward her mother and other people who had impacted her life.

Denial can be a conscious or subconscious decision on the ex-lesbian's part. However, once the Lord has revealed the truth of the matter, we would be wise to respond. Awareness must bring action. Fear can be a great barrier to overcoming denial. It is vital to have a group of people who can support you, pray with you, and encourage you to move through your fear and denial so you can pursue obedience to God.

Grieving

Grieving is a healing process that allows our life to continue after we suffer significant losses. There is much in life to legitimately grieve.

It is right to grieve over sins of omission (not doing things we should do) and commission (doing things we should not do). Our parents may have neglected us emotionally, even if they gave excellent support in a material sense. It is right to grieve the absence of emotional security that we should have received. It is right to grieve the subsequent loss of our childhood when we have been the victim of physical or sexual abuse.

Most of all, we must grieve that our relationships with our family and peers have been broken. Such separations are an everyday part of the sinful world in which we live, and are because of choices we have made. And perhaps the degree of healing we desire will not come about in these relationships—it is okay to grieve that too.

There is another, less obvious area we should feel free to grieve over. When I chose to leave lesbianism in order to follow Christ, I found it hard to grieve the fact that I would never have a female lover again. Why was this so difficult? For a long time I believed that I could not grieve over something that was sinful. I knew lesbianism was wrong in God's sight. Thus, I felt to mourn that loss meant that I was in disagreement with God.

But in reality, that was not the case. I needed to release the sorrow I felt. It was a real emotion and required validation. I found that ignoring this natural process fed my fantasy life. I nourished my long-held dream of finding fulfilment in the arms of another woman because I was not allowing myself to walk through the grief process. To retain that dream was sinful, while the mourning of what I laid aside was not. As I progressed through the stages of grief, I felt able to release that cherished dream. The door to that part of my life was finally closed.

'Those who sow in tears will reap with songs of joy. He who goes out weeping, carrying seed to sow, will return with songs of joy, carrying sheaves with him' (Ps 126:5–6).

Do not rush the grief process. Grieving enables us to recover from the loss and then go on with life. There will be some people who will not respect or allow such grief to take place. They may argue with you or chastise you for going through this process. I encourage you to retain the sense of walking through this process and not to stagnate at this point. There may be a temptation to wallow in your memories rather than seek completion. It is advisable to be accountable to others with regard to this area of healing.

Forgiveness

The giving and receiving of forgiveness is vital to the healing process. The first step is to release God from blame and any expectation or sense of debt we have held against him. We must seek his forgiveness for incorrectly accusing him of wrong-doing. This frees us up to forgive ourselves and others.

Then we need to get in touch with our anger at the person who has wronged us—otherwise our forgiveness will be shallow. We must feel the emotion of anger to break through the denial or minimisation of the wrong done to us. Then, once we are out of the denial stage, we must go into action and implement forgiveness as soon as possible.

It is hard to forgive others if we struggle with pride or selfishness. It takes humility—a willingness to open our lives to God and others—in order to receive forgiveness from God and to bestow it on ourselves and those who have hurt us.

I often hear: 'It's too hard to forgive. After all, just look at what Mum and dad did to me! I have my rights too, you know.' Let us face it—forgiveness *is* hard, but God is within us in this process. And if we do not set the wheels of forgiveness in motion, we will be the ultimate losers.

As well as being sinful, an inability to forgive sets the scene for bitterness, resentment and a chronic mistrust of people and God. Unless she deals with the root cause, the unforgiveness, the woman merely looks for superficial methods of dealing with the problem—a Band-Aid instead of radical surgery. She will find difficulty in relating with people at any depth, and will be subject to compulsive behaviours, such as overeating, workaholism and excessive exercise. These compulsive behaviours are fleshly means of making a woman feel better about herself.

Forgiveness is not a feeling, but a choice. For both Cindy and Alison in chapter 5, forgiveness was something they activated long before they felt like forgiving their mothers.

Many people fear or misunderstand forgiveness. They believe that once forgiveness has occurred, they are to act as though nothing had ever happened. The 'forgive and forget' slogan is not exactly biblical. Even in his resurrected body, Jesus still has the scars in his hands and side as an eternal reminder of his forgiveness of our sins. And God only 'forgets' our sins in as much as he does not count them against us because of our position in Christ. Finally, the Bible is a reminder of people's sins and God's resulting grace, mercy or judgement.

Forgiveness is not synonymous with trust. Forgiveness is required; trust is earned. I must choose to forgive someone, but I have the freedom not to trust that individual again, or to gradually rebuild trust if that seems appropriate.

Trust demands great vulnerability. In order to fully trust, we must know the motivation behind someone's gesture. For instance, when a friend offers to loan me her car, I am secure in the knowledge that she is not imposing a debt system upon me. I do not have to reciprocate in a similar fashion. But if a stranger or acquaintance offered me the loan of a car, I would be suspicious. *What do they want in return?* I would question their motivation for such an act. That suspicion and possible fear would prevent me from accepting their offer.

Therefore, it is important to separate forgiveness from trust. This will give us the freedom to walk in forgiveness without fearing repercussions of such an act.

The issue of forgiveness can bring out another strange

kind of logic that blocks action. It goes something like this:

If I forgive the person who hurt me, then God can't judge or discipline them. They'll be off scott-free. But if I don't forgive the person, then God has the freedom to zap them with judgement! I want justice! Therefore, I will not forgive.

Actually, that whole line of logic derives from a mis-belief about God. The Lord is not limited by whether we forgive or not. He will discipline people or carry out justice as he sees fit. Therefore, our forgiveness does not let people 'off the hook' with God. We are commanded to forgive for our benefit, not necessarily theirs. 'For if you forgive men when they sin against you, your heavenly Father will also forgive you. But if you do not forgive men their sins, your Father will not forgive your sins' (Mt 6:14–15).

Understandably then, we must forgive our mothers for any damaging actions towards us—whether really harm-ful or we just interpreted them that way. In our mind, memories can be minimised or blown out of proportion in relation to the actual incident.

Also, we must seek forgiveness from our mothers for damaging assumptions and attitudes we may have held against them.

After taking steps of forgiveness, be open to God show-ing you a different perspective on the situation between you and your mother.

Confrontation

Confrontation often has such negative connotations that many people avoid entertaining such an idea. But the reality is that some issues do have to be 'aired' before complete healing can take place.

Do we have to face every single person that ever hurt

us? No, I don't believe so. However, we must be open to the Lord's leading in each specific case.

Recognising that confrontation is necessary is one thing, implementing it is something else! I asked Louise how she had approached this issue in her life. (You met Louise in chapter 5—she had the 'best friend' mother.)

'Well, at first I tried to ignore God's promptings,' she answered candidly. 'But, you know, when God starts prodding, there really is no peace unless you respond. So I considered how best to approach my mum.

'At first I thought that a letter would be best. But God made it clear that I was to speak to her. I could see the value of his point. Mum and I had a pretty open relationship. After all, we were best friends!'

'Weren't you frightened?' I asked.

'Frightened, no. Anxious, yes,' laughed Louise. 'It was reassuring to know that God was definitely leading me to this point. I contemplated telephoning her, but again, the Lord made it clear that I had to speak to her in person.'

'So, how did you manage that?'

'Through practice. I spent the next few nights talking to an empty chair in my house. I didn't exactly prepare a speech, but I did want to be clear in my thoughts before approaching her. I needed to know what my responsibility was and what was hers.'

Louise paused, then continued thoughtfully. 'At first, I guess to protect Mum, I took on all responsibility. It was all my fault, but, after a couple of practice sessions, I got a better perspective on the situation. When the big day dawned I felt quietly confident. I'd asked God to prepare Mum to receive what I was going to say. I figured, even if she didn't respond the way I had hoped, at least I had the knowledge I was being obedient to God.'

'And how did it go?' I urged.

Louise thought for a moment and nodded her head slowly up and down. 'Not bad,' she said, 'not bad at all.'

Sometimes, when we ask our mother's forgiveness for particular resentments we have held against her, there may be an opening for more direct communication. The mother may see it as an opportune time to air some of her own thoughts and feelings. This issue should not be forced, however, and every problem does not have to be dealt with all in one conversation!

Reconciliation

Another term for reconciliation is to harmonise. Right now, the thought of finding harmony in your dealings with your mother may appear impossible. It is not. As we saw with Cindy in chapter 5, even death need not be a barrier to reconciliation.

Reconciliation is not an easy or quick act. When your mother is alive, it really does require her co-operation to bring about reconciliation. But that is not your responsibility. You are responsible before the Lord to play your part and leave the complete working out to him. As Paul tells us in the book of Romans: 'Live in harmony with others... In no case paying back evil for evil, determine on the noblest ways of dealing with all people. If possible, so far as it depends on you, live at peace with everyone' (Rom 12:16–18, Modern Language Bible).

We must relinquish our own agenda for reconciliation and our own expectations of what exactly a harmonious relationship will look like. We may never experience those kitchen table chats we always longed for. Mum may never meet us at the front door with a bone-crushing hug. We may never pore over a Laura Ashley catalogue together. To hold on to such dreams is to invite frustration and further the separation between the two of you.

If we maintain God's vision for the relationship and we act in obedience to his prompting, he will not disappoint us.

We can rejoice, too, when we run into problems and trials for we know that they are good for us—they help us learn to be patient. And patience develops strength of character in us and helps us trust God more each time we use it until finally our hope and faith are strong and steady. Then, when that happens, we are able to hold our heads high no matter what happens and know that all is well, for we know how dearly God loves us, and we feel this warm love everywhere within us because God has given us the Holy Spirit to fill our hearts with his love (Rom 5:3–5, TLB).

May the Lord Jesus Christ bless you with a strong sense of his presence with you and his love as you consider his will in your relationship with your mother.

For further study

1. *Homosexuality: A New Christian Ethic* by Elizabeth R Moberly (The Attic Press: USA, 1983) (UK edition: J Clarke, 1983).
2. *Stormie* by Stormie Omartian (Harvest Home: USA, 1986) (UK edition: Kingsway Publications).
3. *Pursuing Sexual Wholeness* by Andrew Comiskey (Creation House: USA, 1989) (UK edition: Monarch Publications: 1990).

CHAPTER SEVEN

MORE ROOTS: FATHER, FAMILY, PEERS AND TRAUMA

Slavery exists in many forms. The Hebrews first entered Egypt as free men, but, over the period of four hundred years, their position changed to that of slave. The home that originally sheltered them became a house of bondage. The sanctuary that once fed and fulfilled them in time of famine now became a source of distress to their souls through the curse of slavery.

Why was this? Their circumstances altered as each new Pharaoh assumed leadership over Egypt. The environment became hostile to the Israelites as one generation followed another. Also, the God of Joseph became a faint memory not only to the Egyptians, but also, it appears, to the Israelites. Intimate worship of God became a thing of the past.

A new mindset gradually developed as successive generations of Hebrews were brought up in slavery. Children of slaves knew no different lifestyle. What they saw and heard—their parents' beliefs and attitudes, their peers and the culture about them—all these things influenced the children. Their past had a definite effect on their present.

Only a radical break with the past could bring the relief they sought and give a positive hope for the future.

What effect has my past had on my present?

You will continue to address this question in stages as your exodus out of lesbianism progresses. There is no set order to the issues that you will need to confront. I may not cover all areas that are pertinent to you as an individual, but many helpful books exist to guide you through specific issues. I encourage you to read them as various areas are discussed.

Daughters and dads

The relationship between a daughter and her father is as important as the relationship between a daughter and her mother.

Beside fostering a sense of security, one of the father's main roles is to affirm his daughter in her femininity. As a representative of the opposite sex, his opinion of his daughter provides affirmation or disapproval in a way that a mother cannot. As the first man a little girl falls in love with, he has the opportunity to nurture her into someone who enjoys her own sexuality. He can allow her to flirt in a safe environment without fear of being rebuffed or taken advantage of.

Dad can bring confidence into his daughter's sense of feminine identity. His correct responses to his girl confirms her sense of being. But a father's incorrect responses can set a girl up for insecurity at the deepest level—in her sense of worth.

An unforgettable night

Susan's eyes filled with tears as she related to me an incident that occurred many years ago. It was the night of her first school dance and she was excited. She even felt good in the dress she was wearing. It wasn't as comfortable as the usual jeans and tee-shirt, but, for once, that didn't matter. Susan looked like a woman, and, more importantly, she felt like one.

Not owning any make-up herself, Susan borrowed her mother's for the night. Application was difficult. *How on earth do women manage to do this every day?* she wondered as she fought courageously with the eyeliner pencil. However, her persistence paid off, and she felt transformed into a 'real' woman. Checking that no one was watching, Susan twirled like a regular beauty queen in front of the full-length mirror.

Timidly, Susan proceeded down the stairs. 'Dad,' she petitioned, 'how do I look?'

Her father glanced up from the evening newspaper, briefly scanned her, then smirked, 'Who hit you in the eyes?'

Her dad may have been teasing, but his words sent her reeling—her budding femininity left in tatters.

Susan remembers running to the bathroom, tears streaming down her cheeks. Once inside, she locked the door and scrubbed her face until it was raw. 'I'll never do that again,' she vowed, knowing that her days of trying to be a woman were over.

Fifteen years later, Susan had still not worn any make-up.

What happened in those brief moments between Susan and her father had a lasting impact. Why? A father's approval or disapproval shapes a girl's image of herself. So, whether he knew it or not, he held tremendous power over her. Susan needed to know from her dad that she was okay. But, after this and other similar incidents, Susan came to the following conclusion: *If Daddy thinks I am worthless, then I must be.*

The result of broken father/daughter relationships

A bad male role model early in life can inhibit a woman from effectively relating to men. As mentioned in chapter 2, a girl can transfer a negative impression of her father directly onto God. This negative transference becomes a barrier to intimacy with God the Father. If we have not received from our earthly Dad a sense of specialness and acceptance for who we are, we can find numerous problems in opening ourselves up to our Heavenly Daddy.

Whether the father/daughter relationship is disturbed through divorce, death or emotional absence, the child develops particular ways of responding to her situation.

Some girls react to inadequate fathering by building up their own sense of the masculine. They emphasise independence, control, duty, and other characteristics at the detriment of the emerging feminine qualities.

Other girls feel overwhelmed by the pain. They are unable to quench their emotions. Indeed, they feel engulfed by them. Instead of fighting the pain, they sink into helplessness, self-pity and depression. They play the victim role to elicit pity, care and love. They demand nurture and exclusive attention from others.

We will look more closely at these issues in a later chapter.

Susan's breakthrough

As we read in chapter 3, Susan finally acknowledged God as her real Father. However, this did not mean that her old ways of relating to God changed overnight. Quite the contrary. In a counselling session, she admitted how difficult it was to overcome her entrenched attitude toward the father figure.

When the word *father* is mentioned, my mental picture is still of someone lost in his own world, oblivious to me or my efforts, ready to put me down with one sarcastic comment. Dad never said that he *didn't* like me. But he never said that he *did* either. Since renouncing those vows I made of self-sufficiency, I now realise how hardened I had become.'

'In what ways?' I asked.

'I had taken the place of God in my own life. I defended myself. I organised my own life. I trusted only my own judgement. I squelched my emotions. In fact, I prided myself on my "logical" thinking. In my mind, being emotional meant being weak, and I had no intention of being weak!

'In retrospect, I'd determined that I wasn't going to need anyone ever again. I was fiercely independent. I knew that I intimidated many people, but it didn't bother me enough to change my ways. If they didn't like me, it was their loss, I reasoned. Work and achievement absorbed me.'

Like many lesbian strugglers, Susan had a successful career. Being praised and valued for what she *did* was some compensation for not being praised and valued for who she *was*.

'So what has changed for you over these past few months?' I quizzed.

Susan seemed deep in thought, then responded. 'Renouncing those vows was only the first step to change. I knew that I had to see God in a new light. If I were to lay down my self-protective shield, I had to know that he was an all-caring God who would protect me as much as or more than I had protected myself.'

'How did you do that?'

'Prayer was important. I asked him to give me a new

and true vision of himself. But I also did word studies using a concordance. I looked up scriptures that included words such as *strength, shield, protector* and *defender.*'

Susan opened her Bible and shared with me some of her favourite passages. 'When I read Psalm 33, especially verses 16 to 21, I realised the trust I had placed in myself and my own attributes.'

No king is saved by the size of his army; no warrior escapes by his great strength. A horse is a vain hope for deliverance; despite all its great strength it cannot save. But the eyes of the LORD are on those who fear him, on those whose hope is in his unfailing love, to deliver them from death and keep them alive in famine. We wait in hope for the LORD; He is our help and our shield. In him our hearts rejoice, for we trust in his holy name (Ps 33:16–21).

'This passage helped me realise how futile trust in self was, and enabled me to refocus onto God, the true source of strength. I began to combat my old beliefs, based on my view of dad, with Psalm 116, verses 5 and 6. This passage demonstrated more of God's true character.'

The LORD is *gracious* and *righteous*; our God is full of *compassion*. The LORD protects the simplehearted; when I was in great need, he saved me (Ps 116:5–6, italics mine).

'As I allowed my wall of protection to slip little by little, God was able to show me why I hid behind it. He showed me that I protected myself using control, independence and my abilities. I guess the abandonment and rejection I'd felt growing up had left me feeling very unprotected. The truth is, I suppressed those negative feelings. What else was I supposed to do?'

Susan's case is not unique. Many woman struggling with lesbianism also reject their softness and sense of vulnerability. They see these not as positive attributes, but as weaknesses that need extinguishing. Consequently, what emerges is a woman who has alienated herself from God's original design. She creates an image that is acceptable to her. She may present herself as being capable, assertive— in fact, almost indestructible! But this image is not true. She is presenting an image that will hide her true self, an image fashioned on past hurts and fear. We will consider this area in chapter 11 on femininity.

Mum and Dad's relationship with each other

How a child sees her parents relating has a lasting impact. If they fail to show affection and attention toward each other, the daughter soon picks up on their subliminal messages.

If the mother is critical and disrespectful of her husband, the daughter may accept that as the normal and correct attitude to have toward all men. If the mother is down-trodden and weak, the girl might reject anything feminine as being 'second class' and not worth embracing.

If the father is abusive to his wife, the little girl may soon learn not to trust men, and will possibly find ways to live without them. If the father leaves his pornography around the house, or leers at the women on television, the child deduces that 'men only want one thing' and may detach herself from any emotionally intimate relating with them.

The relationship the father and mother have with each other is indicative of a broader problem—family dysfunction.

Functional and dysfunctional families

General dysfunction in the house often has a detrimental effect on the children. Most of us come from some kind of dysfunctional family. The only difference is our position on the spectrum of dysfunction. Before examining this concept, let us look at the positive standards God designed for family life.

Norman Wright, a counsellor and author, describes a *functional* family as follows:

- The climate of the home is positive. The atmosphere is basically non-judgemental.
- Each member of the family is valued and accepted for who he or she is. There is regard for individual characteristics.
- Each person is allowed to operate within his or her proper role. A child is allowed to be a child and an adult is an adult.
- Members of the family care for one another and they verbalise their caring and affirmation.
- The communication process is healthy, open and direct. There are no double messages.
- Children are raised in such a way that they can mature and become individuals in their own right. They separate from Mum and Dad in a healthy manner.
- The family enjoys being together. They do not get together out of a sense of obligation.
- Family members can laugh together, and they enjoy life together.
- Family members can share their hopes, dreams, fears and concerns with one another and still be accepted. A healthy level of intimacy exists within the home.[2]

In addition to Wright's list, I would only consider a family to be reasonably functional if Christ is the head of the household and the father is in submission to him.

A *dysfunctional* family follows many unwritten rules. For example, there are taboo subjects that no one mentions: Dad's alcoholism, Mum's mental illness, an unmarried pregnant sister, or cousin James' 'problem' that every-one ignores.

Also, family members are controlled by an overriding motto: 'It's wrong to talk, wrong to feel and wrong to trust.'

Emma

Emma was a product of such an environment. The daughter of an evangelical pastor, she had grown up 'in the church'. Emma was outgoing and congenial. Indeed, her parents referred to her as 'easy-going and carefree'. But that was because of an unwritten rule in their house that no one could express 'negative' emotions—such as disappointment, fear and anger. Consequently, conversation within the family was superficial and always pleasant.

As a little girl, Emma remembers getting angry only once. It was dinner time and she sat at the dining room table, making sure that her eyes remained focused on her plate. Although Emma cannot remember why she was angry, her father's comments remain firmly imprinted in her mind: 'Young lady, go to your room and straighten out your attitude. And don't you come back until you're ready to smile.'

As Emma left the dining room, her mother touched her arm and smiled. 'Come down soon, Emma. We don't want to make Jesus sad, do we?'

Emma no longer sensed her anger as she climbed upstairs. Instead, a wave of guilt swept over the young girl, drowning out the hostility she was feeling. 'I'll never make you sad again, Jesus. I promise,' she sobbed, closing her bedroom door behind her.

At an early age Emma had learned to deny her true feelings. There was no outlet for their expression, therefore it was best that they did not exist at all.

Bridget

Bridget's background differed significantly from Emma's. Bridget was all too aware of her emotions. She loved and hated with equal passion—and bore the emotional and physical scars to prove it.

The family laughingly blamed their passionate tempers on their Irish ancestry and flaming red hair, but alcohol abuse was a way of life to the O'Connors, and it did little to relieve the tension within the house.

Life appeared very unfair to Bridget. In her estimation, her parents saw the elder brothers as absolutely doing no evil. However, Bridget knew the truth to be far different. This sense of injustice gradually built up over a number of years. From her early teens and on into adulthood, Bridget launched a one-woman crusade to negate all that was unfair in life. She trusted no one but herself to look after her affairs. This crusade did not stop at family matters, but continued on into her dealings with others.

Because the initial grievance with her brothers had not been dealt with, hurt and bitterness ate away at Bridget. Soon her life was consumed with 'free-floating' anger bubbling just below the surface, ready to detonate whenever the 'right' circumstances arose.

For both Emma and Bridget, loneliness and isolation had become a way of life.

Emma had many acquaintances, but none she could really call friends. 'People always want more from me than I'm able to give,' she bemoaned. 'They ask me how I am and I have nothing to say. How am I meant to be?'

Bridget's temper always seemed to get the better of her, causing friends to run and hide in fear. 'They just press my buttons and *Pow!*—I explode all over them!'

Neither one of them desired to remain in their present state, but both agreed they felt powerless to change. But the reality is that we can learn to talk, learn to trust, and learn to feel. God provides an environment—his church—

as a place where we can learn to function in a way he designed. Although the church often creates its own problems and fears, it is necessary for us to pursue wholeness within the boundaries that God has laid out for us.

Peer influence on gender identity

Peers include people in such categories as those who are:

1. Our same age.
2. Our same career.
3. Our spiritual or emotional equals.
4. Our schoolmates.

This latter group of childhood peers—our schoolmates—exerts tremendous influence on us during our formative years. With one word or gesture they can express acceptance or rejection which can impact us for the rest of our lives.

In my own childhood, no one called me names or singled me out as being 'strange' or 'queer'. However, I just had this overwhelming sense of being different. This deep knowing that I didn't belong distanced me from others the way name-calling never could.

Although I had girl friends in my pre-teens, I seemed to lose them almost overnight. Whereas I was still content to play soccer and talk about horses with my pre-pubescent buddies, they 'progressed' onto boys. Their waking hours were obsessed with them. The latest teenage heart-throbs and pop idols dominated conversations. This turn of events confused me, but I waited patiently for my time to come.

And I waited.

I was certainly changing. My adolescent emotions, like my classmates, were awakening. But, unlike my girlfriends who focused their attentions on boys, I began looking to women for emotional fulfilment.

The Dutch psychologist, Gerard van den Aardweg, accurately sums up my position at that time:

> If a girl feels slighted as to her mother's affection and under-standing, she can turn to an ideal type of woman possessing in her eyes the desired motherly characteristics: for instance, an easy-going, affectionate teacher, or an older girl with moth-erly attitudes. The self-pitying girl wants the exclusive atten-tion of her idol, clutches to her: 'If only she would give me her love!'[3]

When a girl with lesbian tendencies compares herself to peers of the same sex, she does not, in her own estimation, measure up.

In my judgement I came up 'wanting' in all areas. I was not pretty, slight or feminine. But I did not immediately yield to the inevitable separation. *It's just a phase I'm going through*, I convinced myself. *My time will come*. But, by the age of fifteen, I knew this phase was just not going to pass.

By now I had little in common with any of my former friends. That gap I had perceived in my early teens grew into a gaping chasm. In my opinion there was not, and could never be, a bridge long enough to connect us ever again. From afar I watched them blossom and flower into womanhood. They became 'real' women, while I felt trapped in a 'third sex' mentality. I knew that I was not a man, but I also knew that I did not feel like a woman either.

For other girls who eventually turned to lesbianism, name-calling was very much part of their adolescence. Perhaps this happened because these girls were more expressive than myself. They did not resort to hiding behind a mask of normalcy as I had done, but were more open about their desires.

However extreme their behaviour and dress, name-calling reinforced any questions they may have been struggling with about their sexuality. For some, that provided exactly the 'clarification' they needed to embrace such names as *dyke, lesbo* and *butch*, and label themselves as homosexual. *Even other people notice I'm different*, they reasoned. *Therefore, I must be gay.*

The result is the same, regardless of how a young girl arrives at such a conclusion. There is a parting of the ways between her peers and herself.

For me, this separation emphasised the sense of belonging I felt when I finally entered the lesbian subculture. It had been so long since I had felt connected. Meeting women similar to myself made me feel as though I had come home. I had found my true peer group. Looking back now, I see how needy we all were—a group of misfits who had finally found a niche in life.

Traumatic events

Trauma covers a multitude of areas, such as: emotional abuse, verbal abuse, a death in the family and a daughter's separation from her mother. This separation could be due to divorce, hospitalisation, or even a vacation the mother has taken.

Another major category of trauma is sexual abuse— incest, molestation and rape. Not all people who have been thus victimised become homosexuals, but a conservative estimate shows that approximately eighty per cent of all lesbians have been raped or sexually abused in some way. I know of one ex-gay ministry where this statistic runs closer to ninety-five per cent.

The term sexual abuse covers not only those women who have been abused by men, but also those who have been abused by an older woman or a group of women. This occurrence, although not as common as male/female abuse, certainly exists. Victimisers could be a mother, aunt, teacher, baby-sitter, or a group of older teenage girls out for some 'fun'. If you have survived such abuse, be encouraged. Firstly, you are not alone in your suffering because others have had similar experiences. Secondly, there is healing for you, too, just as for those sexually abused by men.

Traumatic events interfere with a person's very sense of being. Reactions among victims vary greatly, as we saw in chapter 4 with the example of sexual abuse. Some women totally deny that anything took place, while others try to minimise the event's effects on them. Women who have suffered trauma often distrust other people. This may cause them to dictate terms in life in order to retain some sense of control at all times. Inner vows and detachment from others may occur after abuse. Explosive, often unexplained anger can dominate some women's character. For others, compulsive and obsessive behaviours can develop, such as overeating, alcoholism and drug addiction.

When the emotional, verbal or sexual abuser is a man, the girl may fear involvement with all men. Therefore, she grows up avoiding relationships with them at all costs. Even then, as in the case of incest, there can be anger against the mother. Accusations like, 'Why didn't she protect me?' help foster a detachment from the mother. This kind of decision can promote lesbianism as a harbour in which to feel safe and be protected. Response to trauma, to put it very simply, can be overgeneralised, and the victim finds herself hating all men and distrusting all women.

A victim should find a group of people who are able to share and pray together. She may also want to find a good counsellor who specialises in abuse. (See the appendix for information on finding a good counsellor, support group and local church.)

Learning to develop healthy ways of relating to the same and opposite sex also benefits the healing process.

There are many good books for you to read on these issues, which I have listed at the end of this chapter.

Am I bound by my past?

If this is a question that continues to ring in your ears, and you feel overwhelmed with the enormity of the healing process ahead of you, then take courage. God knows you and he is gentle. He places no time limits on your healing. He makes recovery from your past available to you. In *Always Daddy's Girl*, counsellor Norman Wright shares his hope with us.

> What is recovery? It is being able to reflect upon your past and how it contributed to your identity, both positive and negative, without allowing the negative to control your present life. Recovery is finding new meaning to your present life by ridding yourself of the contamination of the past. It means claiming your circumstances instead of letting your circumstances claim your happiness.[4]

As painful as it may appear, we must first recognise those hurtful areas from our past which have coloured our present view on life.

In chapter 6 I mentioned the process of awareness, grieving, forgiveness, confrontation and reconciliation with regard to your mother. You need to apply that same process to your father, family and peers. You need to face traumatic events in your life.

But remember, you are not alone in your healing. Jesus is our ever-present help as we call upon him to walk us through this process. Like Susan, we can run to him and to his word.

'The name of the LORD is a strong tower; the righteous run to it *and are safe*' (Prov 18:10, italics mine).

For further study

Sexual Abuse Resources/Referrals
1. For referrals to Christian counsellors trained to deal with sexual abuse and incest issues, contact:

> Deo Gloria Trust
> Selsdon House
> 212–220 Addington Road
> South Croydon
> Surrey CR2 8LD, UK
> Tel:081 651 6428

> or

> Institute of Biblical Counselling
> Sexual Abuse Ministries
> 16075 West Belleview Avenue
> Morrison, CO 80465, USA
> office phone: (303) 697-5425

2. *A Door of Hope* by Jan Frank (Here's Life Publishers: USA, 1987).
3. *The Wounded Heart: Hope for Adult Victims of Childhood Sexual Abuse* by Dr Dan B Allender (NavPress: USA, 1990).
4. *Helping the Victims of Sexual Abuse* Lynn Heitritter and Jeanette Vought (Bethany House: USA, 1989).

Fathers
1. *Always Daddy's Girl: Understanding Your Father's Impact on Who You Are* by H Norman Wright (Regal Books: USA, 1989).
2. *Daughters Without Dads: Offering Understanding and Hope to Women Who Suffer From the Absence of a Loving Father* by Lois Mowday (Oliver-Nelson: USA, 1990).
3. *Dealing With the Dad of Your Past* by Maureen Rank (Bethany House Publishers: USA, 1990).

Death and Grieving
1. *Someone I Loved Died* by Christian Harder Tangvald (David C Cook: USA, 1988).
2. THEOS (They Help Each Other Spiritually). THEOS publishes an excellent series of magazines which include artwork, poems, journal entries, personal experiences and articles related to grieving the death of a loved one. You can easily apply the principles they cover to grieving over other types of issues. For further information contact:

THEOS
1301 Clark Building
717 Liberty Avenue
Pittsburgh, PA 15222
office phone: (412) 471-7779

Rape
1. *Sexual Violence: The Unmentionable Sin* by Marie Fortune (USA).

Learning in the
Wilderness

CHAPTER EIGHT

EMOTIONAL DEPENDENCY

I first met Sheila at an ex-lesbian support group. A diminutive figure, she perched on the edge of her chair and clutched an oversized bag closely to her chest. Her discomfort was obvious to all. Sheila listened closely while I taught, but offered no explanation for her presence at the meeting.

That night's teaching addressed the subject of emotional dependency. Throughout the meeting I shared some of the following concepts.

The term *lesbianism* covers three categories of women. First are those women who strive to fulfil sexual desires and emotional needs through other women. The second group have not acted out sexually, but have sought completion through an emotional relationship with another woman. The third category of lesbians are those who were too frightened to act upon their desires, so they resort to fantasy.

Although one can engage in emotional dependency and never experience a homosexual thought, emotional dependency frequently precedes lesbian sexual activity.

Co-dependency versus emotional dependency

Emotional dependency is not synonymous with co-dependency, and neither approaches anything close to healthy relationships. A classic co-dependent relationship involves one partner with a life-dominating addiction, such as to alcohol, drugs, gambling, food, work or sex. The co-dependent partner completely revolves his or her life around the addicted person and their addiction.

The *active* co-dependent attempts to rescue her partner from the addiction by hiding the booze or locking him or her out of the house. The *passive* co-dependent enables the partner to continue in the addiction by paying the gambling bills, making excuses for her partner's behaviour, or ignoring the problem.

Either way, the co-dependent person is an efficient manager of people and things around her. However, she rarely takes care of her own needs. In co-dependency, the core of the relationship is the addiction.

An emotionally dependent relationship usually involves two people who are completely enmeshed in each other's lives. Emotional dependency can also be a one-sided affair. The idolised person can be totally oblivious to the feelings of another. When two people are involved in dependent behaviour, neither party can distinguish their own personal boundaries and life from the personhood of the other. In emotional dependency, the core of the relationship is the relationship itself.

In contrast, an emotionally healthy relationship consists of two people who know who they are as individuals. There is a mutual desire to seek the Lord's best for the other and not a preoccupation to get one's own needs met. We will explore healthy relating in chapter 10. In a healthy friendship, the core of the relationship is the Lord.

Am I emotionally dependent?

Questions to ask oneself concerning a friendship[5]:

1. Do I experience frequent jealousy, possessiveness, and a desire for exclusivism in my relationship?
2. Do I view other people as a threat to my special friendship?
3. Is it my preference to be alone with my friend rather than in the company of others?
4. Do I become irrational, angry or depressed if I sense my friend is withdrawing from me?
5. Am I losing interest in all other relationships?
6. Do I experience romantic or sexual feelings about this person?
7. Do I become preoccupied with this person's appearance, personality, problems and interests as our relationship develops?
8. Am I unwilling to make short-term or long-term plans that do not include my friend?
9. Am I able to see my friend's faults realistically?
10. Do I become defensive when asked about our friendship?
11. Do I display physical affection which is inappropriate for a friendship, such as making sure we always have physical contact while sitting on the couch together and talking?
12. Do I find myself speaking freely *for* her in conversations?
13. Do others feel uncomfortable around us when I act in this way towards my friend?

If you are answering 'yes' to some of these questions, there is every chance that you have one or more friendships that are out of keel.

Emotionally dependent—emotionally distressed

Sheila was quite shaken by the subject addressed in the meeting. Although not willing to speak that night, she agreed to a private appointment with me.

Sheila arrived promptly at my office the next morning. As she made herself comfortable, I noticed that her eyes were red and puffy. She had obviously been crying.

'How can I help you?' I volunteered, as I plugged in the coffee pot.

Sheila shifted nervously in her chair. 'This is so embarrassing, Jeanette. You see, I'm married with two children...'

Her voice trailed off as she stared at the wall, groping for the right words to say. 'My husband, David, is a pastor and I help him out by counselling some of the women who come for help.'

'Is that a problem?' I asked.

She nodded. 'Well, six months ago this young woman, Amy, came to our home. She told me that she had come from a lesbian background, hadn't known the Lord long, and desired further discipleship. I was happy to help her and, in turn, she looked after the children while David and I went to meetings or social events. Everything was fine. She would even pop in just to chat, especially on the evenings David had to work late. Other days we'd go shopping together. We had so much in common. From the onset it was as though we had known each other for years.' She hesitated. 'Then one day, out of the blue, Amy announced that she was changing churches and would be going to a group discipleship meeting at her new church.'

'How did you feel?' I probed. I sensed Sheila needed to know that I was sensitive to her predicament.

Sheila shrugged as she looked down at her lap. 'I was confused and hurt, wondering what I had done wrong. But more importantly, I was frightened. The thought of losing Amy's friendship was incomprehensible to me.'

I asked Sheila to describe what types of things she was thinking at the time. She responded, 'Thoughts flashed through my mind, like: *I can't live without Amy. She understands me. I understand her. She makes me feel worthwhile. She needs me to nurture her.* The more I considered Amy's role in my life, the more I realised how enmeshed our two lives had become. Then I considered David. I loved him deeply, and yet I felt estranged from him. Amy filled a void in my life that David never could. The feelings I had for him didn't match the intensity I felt for her.'

Handing Sheila a cup of coffee, I asked, 'Did you tell Amy about your feelings for her?'

'No, I was scared that I might frighten her away. But I noticed that my behaviour changed around her. The carefree attitude that I once had towards Amy disappeared. I began to be possessive of our friendship. I didn't like it when she would tell me about the fun times she'd had at a singles event in her new church. I became suspicious of other women, fearing that they were more interesting to Amy than I was, and would come between our friendship.'

'What did you do to keep Amy's interest?'

Methods of manipulation

Sheila blushed at my question and looked at me sheepishly. 'I manipulated my way into a deeper relationship with her. I would mail her little cards telling her how important our friendship was to me. The 'hello' and 'goodbye' hugs between us got longer and more intense. And I would make little comments over the phone that produced guilt in Amy.'

I was intrigued by Sheila's disclosure. 'Give me an example,' I urged.

'Well, I'd let her talk about some fun that she'd had with her friends. Then I would sigh and tell her in an "accepting" tone that I understood her desire to be around single people. After all, they are more fun to be with than a married woman with children!'

I smiled, recalling my own past manipulative methods. 'How did she react to that kind of statement?'

'At first she would try to pacify me by immediately suggesting that we do something together. But after several weeks that method no longer worked. Then I thought I would play the "hard to get" role. I made excuses why Amy and I couldn't get together. I cited David or the children as needing me more. I also cut short our telephone conversations so that she always hung up feeling frustrated. I hated what I was doing but I knew that this would keep her tagging along. By this time I was prepared to resort to anything in order to keep her interest.'

'Even sleep with her?'

My direct question rocked Sheila. 'Well, er, well,' she stammered, fighting gallantly to restore some composure. 'I've never considered sleeping with another woman in my life before.'

Sheila paused and breathed deeply. 'But I felt so powerless and in need of Amy's love, that I actually considered that possibility. I don't know if I would have carried it out if she'd suggested it. But I certainly didn't dismiss the thought either.'

'How was your relationship with David at this time?'

'He knew something was going on with me, Jeanette, but he never suspected anything wrong in my friendship with Amy. In fact, David encouraged our times together, saying how pleased he was that I had finally found a close friend. Up to this point he'd been worried that I was too shy to make deep friendships with other women.'

Sheila fumbled in her bag for a tissue and wiped her eyes. 'You know, in the back of my mind I wanted David to question me about my feelings towards Amy. I felt incapable of getting myself out of the mess I was in. I *wanted* David to find out. I knew that this was all wrong.'

There was a pause in the conversation as Sheila quietly sobbed. Her pent-up pain was finally finding release. Tenderly, I looked at Sheila. 'How is your relationship with the Lord?' She smiled weakly. 'What relationship? This whole six-month period has been like a see-saw. As my feelings for Amy intensified, my love and dependence on God decreased. I couldn't concentrate on him. Even in the midst of singing worship songs in church, I found my thoughts wandering towards Amy. *What is she doing now? Who is she with? What will she be doing after her church service?* I really sensed that I was losing God in the midst of this relationship. Now I'm at the end of my tether. I want Amy.'

Sheila stopped and sighed. 'But I want God more. As painful as this process is going to be, I do want to get right with God. I know that Amy can never successfully fill his place. More importantly, I know that I shouldn't be looking for someone else to take his place in my life. I don't know how I got myself into this mess.'

For the first time during our talk, Sheila met my gaze. Her reddened eyes looked desperately at me. 'Jeanette, can you help me?'

I shared the following principles with her.

What is dependency?

Another name for sinful dependency occurs frequently in the Bible. That word is *idolatry*. Idolatry occurs when we place someone or something before God. They or it become the objects of worship. In her book, *The Broken Image*, Leanne Payne addresses this issue by reminding us that we are creatures of worship. We will either worship the Creator or the created. Romans 1:25 illustrates this point: 'They exchanged the truth of God for a lie, and worshipped and served created things rather than the Creator.'

Indulging in idolatry enslaves us to our passions. We base our decisions on our feelings and desires instead of exhibiting the fruit of the Spirit as found in Galatians 5:22: 'But the fruit of the Spirit is love, joy, peace, patience, kindness, goodness, faithfulness, gentleness and self-control. Against such things there is no law.'

When we are steeped in dependency, we are vulnerable to hatred, jealousy, rage and selfish ambition (seeking to get our own needs met). These and other emotions are described in Galatians 5:21 as 'acts of the sinful nature'.

The golden calf

The Israelites, too, were prone to idolatry. They waited at the foot of Mount Sinai while Moses received the law from God. Everything seemed relatively peaceful for the first thirty-eight days, but the Hebrews became increasingly tired of waiting for Moses to return, weary of waiting for the promised land, and indifferent to God's agenda. They took decision-making into their own hands.

The Hebrews impatiently demanded a god to go before them into Canaan *now* instead of waiting for God's timing and God's method. They willingly gave up their gold to make an idol cast in the shape of a golden calf. Worship of the calf soon degenerated into a full-fledged orgy, and thoughts of God vanished from their minds.

'But our fathers refused to obey him. Instead, they rejected him and *in their hearts turned back to Egypt'* (Acts 7:39, italics mine). 'But they rebelled against me and would not listen to me; they did not get rid of the vile images they had set their eyes on, nor did they forsake the idols of Egypt' (Ezek 20:8).

Are you weary from waiting on the Lord to minister to your needs? Have you chosen your own ways over God's way? You may have walked away from *sexual* relationships, but have you clung on to *emotionally dependent* relationships as a compromise? Do you love the Lord with your whole heart, mind and strength, or are there pockets of idolatry left in your life? Does your heart periodically return to Egypt?

If so, God has graciously provided a way of escape from the snare of dependency.

Recognising the roots of dependency

As with other forms of destructive behaviour, knowing why we do something can help us overcome the problem. Emotional dependency does not occur in a vacuum. Many of the roots of dependency are similar to those of lesbianism:

- Real or perceived rejection from significant others
- Unfilled need for love and approval from members of the same sex
- Rejection of feminine role and gender
- Low self-esteem
- Failure or unwillingness to accept maturity/adulthood—a retreat to an earlier, more secure stage of life
- Need to be in control (this is easier to achieve in same-sex relationships)
- Mistrust—safer to set up the world the way we want it than to accept what God has planned for us
- Loneliness, which tends to breed insecurity
- Anger or bitterness towards the opposite sex
- Frustration or disillusionment with opposite-sex relationships
- Rebellion—not willing to surrender areas of our life to God

It is not necessary for you to have *all* of the above

problems to be struggling with emotional dependency, but you may well identify with some of those areas.

Confession of sin

The first step to breaking free from the bondage of dependency is to confess it as sin. In my own life I have certainly not been immune from dependent relationships. Up until a few years ago, I didn't even know there was any other way of relating to people! When a Christian friend pointed out the idolatry factor to me, I immediately rationalised my sin. Mental arguments with God ensued. *Haven't I given up enough already? You can't possibly want me to live without friends. But we genuinely like each other!*

But God was persistent in showing me his standard for my life. In a bizarre way I used to enjoy the peaks and valleys emotional dependency offered. The roller-coaster ride of living on the highs and denying the lows fed my craving for immediate excitement. But emotional dependency became an increasingly heavy burden as I recognised it being in direct opposition to God's desire for me.

Obedience became the crucial factor to healing. Even though I was semi-blind to the destructiveness of dependent relationships, I chose to follow God's directive and declare my actions and feelings as sinful. Eventually this enabled me to see how injurious they were to my relationship with God.

Recognising God's position

God showed me through various incidents that I was ruling my own life. I saw personal needs and chose *my own* methods of satisfying them. I would vacillate between emotional isolation—remaining detached from everyone and everything—and dependency—over-attachment to one person. Dependency would occur when loneliness overwhelmed me. I became desperate for the sense of love, security and belonging that another woman could offer me. The problems of loneliness will be discussed in chapter 9.

The next step in overcoming dependency is to recognise God as being central to our existence, and allow him to take his rightful place in our lives. This is easier to say than do. It requires self-discipline to filter *all* our thoughts, desires and emotions through him. But dependence on God produces a firm foundation on which we can experience intimacy and security, not only with him, but also with others.

Developing intimacy

Another step in the right direction occurs as we shatter the idolatrous myth of instant intimacy and begin to develop real intimacy.

'I feel I've known you all of my life!' How often have you spoken or heard that line, believing every syllable uttered?

'Instant intimacy' often results from mutual needs in the two participants. Stressful situations serve as a breeding ground for making this mistake. In our quest to fill our emotional void, we ignore personal boundaries and lose any true perspective on the relationship. In such instances, we may desire intimacy but settle for enmeshment.

True intimacy does not spring upon us in the space of a few hours. Irrespective of what our emotions sometime tell us, it can take years to build a deep relationship. It also requires work and commitment to seek the best for another. True emotional closeness does not occur if we are obsessed with meeting our own needs.

In order to overcome our dependency on others, we need to develop intimacy with God. That requires time spent in his company, whereby he enables us to receive a deeper revelation of himself, and of his love for us.

True intimacy can be a very frightening prospect. Many believe it is safer to keep God at arm's length, rather than risk being vulnerable with him. We fear hurt and loss of control if we throw ourselves on God's mercy. Many of us do not know *how* to receive love because, in order to receive, we have to be able to trust. We can only trust someone if we know the motivation behind their action. However, we can only know a person's true motivation if we are intimate with that person. Thus, a *'Catch-22'* situation occurs if we function according to our feelings. As with most of our interactions with God, we need to choose fact over feeling. We need to walk in faith.

Moses—model of intimacy with God

Moses was such a man who walked by faith. The time he spent on Mount Sinai was in a close, personal relationship with God. Not only did God speak to Moses face to face (Ex 33:11), but also mouth to mouth (Numbers 12:8, RSV).

In his book, *Enjoying Intimacy with God*[6], J Oswald Sanders describes four levels of intimacy with God that occurred at Mount Sinai.

The Hebrew people reached the first level of intimacy. They assembled at the foot of the mountain, but were forbidden to touch Mount Sinai, on pain of death. Their intimacy with God was limited because they saw only one facet of God's character. 'To the Israelites the glory of the LORD looked like a consuming fire on top of the mountain' (Ex 24:17).

Their lack of intimacy soon became apparent when they replaced worship of God with idolatrous worship of a calf.

The priests and elders of Israel attained the second levels of intimacy as they ascended part way up the mountain. 'But God did not raise his hand against these leaders of the

Israelites; they saw God, and they ate and drank' (Ex 24:11). They obviously had fellowship with God and with each other. Moses was confident that they could lead Israel in his absence when he ascended higher up the mountain. Unfortunately, the relationship which the priests and elders had with God did not stand under testing. Aaron not only allowed idolatry to take place among the people, he actually instigated the collection of the gold in order to make the calf (Ex 32:2). Interestingly, Nadab and Abihu, who also ascended the mountain, were later killed as a direct result of their disobedience to God (Lev 10:2). Although all had experienced a revelation of God, the experience had obviously *not* been life-changing.

Joshua alone achieved the third level of intimacy. He ascended far higher than anyone else, other than Moses. Elsewhere in the book of Exodus, we find that Joshua had a desire to remain in the Lord's presence. 'Then Moses would return to the camp, but his young aide Joshua son of Nun *did not leave the tent*' (Ex 33:11, italics mine).

Moses was the only one to reach the top of the mountain and achieve true intimacy with God. Even then he could not comprehend the fullness of God and had to hide in the crevice of a rock. To see God was to die. The effect of Moses' encounter with God showed on his face, shone as a reflection of God's glory. Thus, Moses' relationship with God was obvious to all. 'When Aaron and all the Israelites saw Moses, his face was radiant, and they were afraid to come near him' (Ex 34:30).

Jesus and intimacy

Jesus also had various levels of personal closeness with those around him. There were the crowds who sought out Jesus to hear him teach and see him perform miracles. Then he had seventy-two followers who preached and taught in his name (Lk 10:1). Then there were the twelve disciples who received three years of training directly from Jesus. Among those twelve were three—Peter, James and John—who enjoyed an intimate relationship with Christ. And from among those three there was one—John—who described himself as 'the disciple whom Jesus loved' (Jn 13:23).

Although we may see this as a presumptuous statement for John to make, it shows his ability to appropriate all that Jesus had to offer him. He recognised the love Jesus had for him and welcomed it without reservation. This enabled John to love others with the same intensity of love that he himself had received.

What about us?

The Bible clearly states that God shows no favouritism (Acts 10:34). He does not desire one of us over another, but desires intimacy with each of us. The choice is ours. We can become as intimate with Jesus as we choose to be.

Using the Old Testament analogy of God on Mount Sinai, the path up the mountain to intimacy with God is steep and rugged. There is a temptation to stay at the lower level where the paths are smoother and the going is easy. However, those paths are misleading. Dependency on people, objects and careers lies at the end of these other paths. But if we desire true intimacy with God we will persevere upward, even when the ground is rough and the weather is unsettled. When we focus our eyes on the top of the mountain—Jesus—we will not give a second thought to alternative, easier pathways.

Sheila's breakthrough

Sheila and I met weekly for a period of time. She made some general progress, but I sensed the need to address more specific issues.

'Sheila, now that we have spent the past few weeks looking at your need for intimacy with God, I want us to spend some time looking at other relationships in your life. How much time do you spend with your husband, David?'

She sat and reflected for a few moments. 'David is the only pastor in our church. He's so conscientious about his work that he is away most evenings attending various meetings.'

I smiled. 'Sheila, that doesn't answer my question. How much time do you spend with David?'

A hint of frustration clouded her face. 'Although Saturday is supposed to be family day, David often excuses himself early afternoon to put "finishing touches" to his sermon for the next day.'

I leaned forward in my chair. 'Is that the only day he has off?'

'Oh, no,' Sheila answered quickly. 'We have Wednesday too.' She paused. 'But that is often eaten away by distraught parishioners demanding "just a few words" with the pastor. I find myself resenting David for taking those calls. He sounds so caring and loving on the phone, but I feel taken for granted.'

Her last comment interested me. 'What do you mean by that?' I queried.

Sheila took a deep breath and blurted. 'I know he's under stress, but so am I! I have two boys aged three and four who need a dad. I need a husband. I feel as though I am a single mother half of the time. He cares for his parishioners more than he cares for me. He is always talking about Mr so-and-so needing this and that. What about me? I need things too, you know!'

As she talked about her relationship with her husband, I could see how she was primed for a dependent relationship. When Amy arrived on the scene, she offered Sheila her time, along with much-needed practical help, and emotional support. She was there when Sheila needed a shoulder to cry on, or a sympathetic ear to hear her problems. She was available when David was not. Amy filled a very large hole in Sheila's life.

I let Sheila cry for a while. She had suppressed her anger and hurt for a number of years. By recognising it and verbally releasing some of her emotions, Sheila was now beginning her walk along the path to recovery.

The recovery process

She had to lay down some ground rules if she was to overcome this devastating emotional dependency. First, I gently but strongly recommended she consider telling the truth to David. He needed to know how Sheila felt about him and about their situation.

Later that week, she did tell David about her relationship with Amy. Although he was shocked and upset about this disclosure, he committed himself to Sheila's healing. As they both sought the Lord over the next couple of months, God showed them practical measures they could take to improve their marriage which would benefit the whole family.

Sheila understood that she needed to look at the deeper issues which had promoted dependency in the first place. This was painful at times, but, with the support of a small group, Sheila allowed God to highlight areas, such as her feelings and desires, which she had closed off to him in the past.

Eventually, Amy also recognised her need for help. She continued to attend her new church and was able there to establish accountability within a small group of women.

Both Amy and Sheila desired a godly friendship with each other, but they recognised that there is always a cost to violating God's concept of friendship. Therefore, they took concrete steps to reduce the temptations to get enmeshed again. Sheila and Amy had no contact in the initial stages of healing. This helped both women focus on the Lord and not on each other.

After six months, they began to see each other again, although they limited contact to social events involving other people. Whatever their relationship may be in the future, both realise that under God's direction it will not be the same destructive relationship they allowed to develop the first time.

There is no set formula to the healing process from emotional dependencies. While God led Sheila and Amy into a relationship of occasional social contact, he may lead some of us to permanently break our contact with former partners in emotional dependency.

We may not initially like the idea of cutting back or completely breaking off such relationships. Some women argue, 'But God is a God of reconciliation, so why can't I continue in this friendship?' True, God calls us to reconcile relationships, but we must not use that as an excuse to continue in an idolatrous emotional dependency. God repeatedly calls himself a jealous God.

> I am the LORD your God, who brought you out of the land of Egypt, out of the house of slavery. You shall have no other gods before me. You shall not make for yourself an idol... You shall not worship them or serve them; for I, the LORD your God, am a jealous God... (Ex 20:2–5, NASB).

Nothing in our life should violate the primacy of our relationship with him.

First we must reconcile ourselves with God, and then with partners from previous emotional dependencies— *only if and when God clearly leads us to do so.*

Thus, the most important factor in this whole process is co-operation with the Holy Spirit. He will ultimately lead you into healing. There is no strict time frame within which the Holy Spirit must work. What may take six months for one woman, can take six years for another. By yielding our agenda and expectations to God, we are released to be obedient to his ways.

Again, the choice to break free from old methods of relating is strictly ours. The book of Jonah warns us about the consequence of not dealing with this issue. 'Those who cling to worthless idols forfeit the grace that could be theirs' (Jon 2:8).

But God does not force us to face this problem of overcoming dependency alone. 'So do not fear, for I am with you; do not be dismayed, for I am your God. I will strengthen you and help you; I will uphold you with my righteous right hand' (Is 41:10).

There is a time in our healing which calls for us to be 'emotionally celibate' and to withdraw from heavy emotional involvement with others. In my own life, I found that I was largely ignorant of healthy ways of relating to other people. By extracting myself from emotional dependencies, I opened the door to loneliness. Loneliness is not necessarily a negative emotion. I will share in the next chapter how it gave me ample opportunity to focus my emotions on God.

For further study

1. *Healing for Damaged Emotions* by David A Seamands (Victor Books: USA, 1988) (UK edition: Scripture Press, 1986).
2. *Emotional Dependency: A Threat to Close Relationships* by Lori Thorkelson Rentzel (Exodus International: USA, 1987).
3. *Enjoying Intimacy with God* by J Oswald Sanders (Moody Press: USA, 1980).

CHAPTER NINE

LONELINESS

I lay sprawled across the living room carpet for the better part of the evening, drawing myself to an upright position only to pour another shot of Scotch. It was my twenty-sixth birthday. I held up my glass and toasted myself for the umpteenth time that night. 'Happy birthday, Jeanette. May you have many more as boring as this one!'

I recalled my birthday of the previous year. As far as my memory served me, it had been boisterous and fun. I had felt loved and cared for by my friends. I reminisced over the dinner party for ten in a Persian restaurant followed by a romantic late night for two. I sighed deeply. Tonight was certainly different. Without a doubt, I was still having a party. Only this time it was a colossal pity party thrown and attended by yours truly.

It had been nine months since my conversion—nine months since I had separated myself from my gay friends. That night, for the first time, I felt the full impact of my decision. Loneliness had become my closest friend. Although I had made acquaintances with those at church, my 'secret problem' prevented me from true intimacy

143

with them. I felt chained to my past, not knowing that I held the key to my release.

Freedom and friends would come eventually. First, however, I had to learn to rely on God's ability to comfort and sustain me through the difficult times and the initial loneliness after leaving lesbianism.

Nothing new under the sun

Loneliness is not some new phenomenon created by modern man. We can trace it back to our first ancestor, Adam.

Even though past woundings may have sent us scurrying into our self-protective shell, we are social creatures by nature. God proclaimed that fact in Genesis 2:18: 'The LORD God said, "It is not good for the man to be alone."' '

Although Adam had an intimate relationship with God, God still deemed it necessary for Adam to have human contact, and thus provided Eve for him. Sadly, sin entered the picture and distorted God's intention for relationships. Disobedience by Adam and Eve led to a separation between them and God, and an estrangement from each other. Separation from God, the source of love, and from our fellow man, breeds loneliness. Sin heralded the arrival on earth of fear, accusation, defensiveness, guilt and rejection—all of which reinforce an individual's sense of isolation.

Prior to the Fall, Adam and Eve were unconscious of self. Sin drastically altered this state and they became aware of their own nakedness, producing shame. 'He answered, "I heard you in the garden, and I was afraid because I was naked; so I hid"' (Gen 3:10).

Today, we struggle with the same problem. Sin separates. Self-centredness enters the picture as a woman ceases to focus on God, rejects his role in her life and attempts to meet her own needs. Self-consuming thoughts beset a woman. *What's in it for me? How am I affected by this action?*

She fails to ask what benefit she can be to others and is preoccupied with what they can do for her.

Sin breeds sin. It hinders our reconciliation with God. However, many Christians are also paralysed by a sense of guilt which they carry around like a favourite backpack. This extra burden keeps them from running the race at God's intended pace (see Hebrews 12:1).

Guilt—the gift that keeps on giving

If we have repented of our sins and have asked God to forgive us—*he has done so*. Christians are so often burdened by guilt because they have not forgiven themselves. Often we don't *feel* forgiven and come to the incorrect conclusion it is because we are *not* forgiven. Our subjective thoughts override any objectivity we may have once had on the subject. These thoughts are the product of a faulty belief that forgiveness is a feeling when, in reality, living in forgiveness is a choice.

The consequences of not forgiving ourselves can be far-reaching. As we replay our sins over in our minds, we replay our guilt. Consequently, we imprison ourselves spiritually by our unbelief.

To walk in guilt is to walk in uncertainty. Therefore, we are unsure of where we stand with God. The truth of the word is lost as we deem ourselves guilty, and therefore, we also render ourselves worthless. Consequently, we place low expectations on God because we don't expect him to listen to a worthless person.

A clear distinction has to be made. In truth, we are unworthy to receive Christ and the gift of salvation that he offers us. However, we do have worth. Consider this example. When I buy a car, I pay the price that is usually compatible to its worth, perhaps £10,000. God paid the full price for our salvation, and the price for forgiveness of sin is high—the death of Jesus Christ. We are of worth because of the price he paid, and not because of anything we did, or did not do.

If we are walking under a cloud of guilt, we deprive ourselves of the things that God wants us to enjoy, like the ability to walk in wholeness. When we decide whether or not we are worthy to receive his blessings, we are placing ourselves in the position of God. But how can we ever decide if and when we are worthy enough? Who establishes the pass or fail mark? We do. Now that *is* a sin and we must repent.

Living under a cloud of guilt undermines our ability to function according to the truth. Therefore, we sabotage any chance of true intimacy with others. Guilt encourages a fear of rejection. *If people really knew me, they wouldn't like me. Therefore, I must not disclose who I really am.*

The consequence of hiding ourselves

As a fairly new Christian, I presented an acceptable image to my new friends at church. This was not done intentionally to deceive them, but to protect myself. However, the longer I presented myself as a perfectly normal church member, the harder it became for me to develop close friends. I hid behind a mask, while my true thoughts, struggles and feelings never surfaced in my interactions with friends. Without appropriate honesty in my relationships, I had dug myself into a hole from which I saw no way out.

Fear of rejection walked hand in hand with pride. I was ashamed of my past sin and too proud to admit my sin to others. I deftly fielded questions about boyfriends and marriage. Initially that was easy because I was used to such deception, but gradually my sins of omission began to weigh heavily on me. I used humour as a shield against any penetrating questions thrown my way, and my sarcasm served as fiery darts to counter-attack those who persisted in 'getting to know me'. In short, I built an impregnable fortress. But in locking people out, I also locked myself in. As fear of being known increased in intensity, loneliness dominated my life.

Was I a freak? Certainly not. I was not alone in my loneliness. As I have since found out, many ex-lesbians have suffered with the same problem.

Loneliness is a spiritual problem

Recently, Carol, my co-worker, shared with me how she had tackled this dilemma.

'Overcoming loneliness was one of the hardest areas for me to address,' she said. 'I remember the time I determined to leave my dependent relationship once and for all in order to follow God. I did all the right things, gave back the presents my friend had given me. I destroyed photographs, books, cards and sentimental mementos.' Carol looked at me. 'You know what I mean?'

I nodded. *Only too well!* I thought.

Carol continued. 'I kept myself busy for the first week. I did anything that would keep me out of the apartment. But when I would finally return home late at night, reality would hit me. There was no one there to smile or greet me. Even the cat was apathetic to my homecoming!

'I remember collapsing onto the sofa one night and sinking into a full-blown depression. I was confused. I knew I was being obedient to God when I broke off the relationship, so I didn't understand my negative emotional response. I thought that I would be elated or feel something that was at least halfway pleasant during this process. But my "reward" was an overwhelming sense of loneliness.'

'What did you do?'

Carol laughed. 'Well, I dabbled with self pity for a

while, until even *I* became sick of myself! I felt there was no one I could talk to, no one who would understand.

'Then I remembered God. A couple of weeks back I'd heard a sermon about the loneliness of Jesus. The pastor spoke about how Jesus' friends had abandoned him at Gethsemane when he needed them most. But more importantly, he talked about the loneliness Jesus experienced during his separation from God at the crucifixion. For the first time in his life, Jesus' relationship with his heavenly Father was severed. This was a direct consequence of taking the full weight of the world's sin.'

Carol opened up her Bible and read to me Matthew 27:46: 'About the ninth hour Jesus cried out in a loud voice, *"Eloi, Eloi, lama sabachthani?"* '—which means, 'My God, my God, why have you forsaken me?'

Carol looked up from the page. 'Although I had read that verse numerous times before, that night the reality of Christ's separation from God hit me. As I contemplated that thought, gradually the realisation that I had access to God dawned on me. If Christ experienced loneliness, being separated from God, then surely I would find solace being in relationship with God.'

'But weren't you already a Christian at that point?' I interrupted.

'Oh, yes,' answered Carol, 'but I'd never seen God in that role. Even though I could quote verses regarding his love and care for me, I doubted the truth that he could fulfil this particular need. Now I realised that I had a way of combatting loneliness—through entering into a deeper relationship with God.'

'What did you do first?'

Carol smiled. 'I did what I have to do every time I realise more about God.'

'What's that?'

'Surrender!'

Victory through surrender

We must surrender our 'right' to offset loneliness in our own way. Many of us have used drugs, alcohol, people, careers and simple activity to fill that aching void. God asks us to abandon our well-worn—but ultimately useless—methods to him. Through the surrender of our agenda we are able to see and accept reality, that life is out of our control. We have the choice to trust him or continue to trust ourselves. Leaving the outcome of our lives in God's hands is a frightening prospect if we are not intimate with the Lord. But to follow his leading will create that fellowship we have longed for, first with him, and second with his people.

Elisabeth Elliot says:

> With what misgivings we turn our lives over to God, imagining somehow that we are about to lose everything that matters. Our hesitancy is like that of a tiny shell on the seashore, afraid to give up the teaspoonful of water it holds lest there not be enough in the ocean to fill it again. Lose your life, said Jesus, and you will find it. Give up, and I will give you all. Can the shell imagine the depth and plenitude of the ocean? Can you and I fathom the riches, the fullness of God's love?[7]

Not long after my twenty-sixth birthday, I learned this important lesson. By relinquishing my self-protective mask and allowing my true self to be exposed, I had the freedom to love and to be loved in return. Relinquishment allowed God full reign in my life. Opening that door to him ushered me into the next step of my healing. What was the next step? A walk into 'no man's land'—a seemingly arid desert of healing. Only later could I savour the relational milk and honey of the promised land.

Combating loneliness—a walk in the wilderness

We may be tempted to skirt around the desert in our pursuit of healing. After all, who wants pain and hardship? We may desire a tree-lined boulevard, well lit with clear directions posted every half mile. But that is not God's way. His healing path is narrow and sometimes seems non-existent to the naked eye. In God's mind we need the uncertainty of the desert, the sandstorms and the ever-changing terrain to bring us to the point of abandoning ourselves to him.

> Therefore I am now going to allure her; I will lead her into the desert and speak tenderly to her. There I will give her back her vineyards, and will make the Valley of Achor [trouble] a door of hope. There she will sing as in the days of her youth, as in the day she came up out of Egypt (Hos 2:14–15).

Remember, God did not intend the Hebrews to wander around the desert for forty years. His intention was to bring them through the desert and into his blessing. Disobedience turned what could have been just a two-week hike into a forty-year trudge!

The desert has its blessings, for in the wilderness we become sensitive to God's word, his tender word. In the heat of the desert God gives us hope and joy. God is just as concerned with the journey as he is with its outcome. When the sand begins to choke you and a refreshing oasis appears a long way off, be encouraged. God has not abandoned you but is working on your character.

> Dear [sisters], is your life full of difficulties and temptations? Then be happy, for when the way is rough, your patience has a chance to grow. So let it grow, and don't try to squirm out of your problems. For when your patience is finally in full bloom, then you will be ready for anything, strong in character, full and complete (Jas 1:2–3, TLB).

Both Carol and I found that loneliness was a companion during the early part of our walk out of lesbianism. For me, it was tempting to grumble at God and to rectify the problem using my own methods. Were Carol and I walking a previously untrodden path? No. Four thousand years ago, the Hebrews had to learn similar lessons.

Life without McDonalds!

The Hebrews had been walking in the desert for six weeks. By now the excitement of leaving the bondage in Egypt was beginning to wear thin. Were the Israelites encouraged by the miracles they had witnessed over the past few months? Did they stand in awe at the ten plagues, or the parting of the Red Sea, or the transformation of the bitter water into sweet water?

'If only we had died by the LORD's hand in Egypt! There we sat around pots of meat and ate all the food we wanted, but you have brought us out into this desert to starve this entire assembly to death' (Ex 16:3).

Such gratitude! In his infinite mercy, God sent manna from heaven for the Israelites to eat. This was a divine provision, but they had to gather it daily themselves. God laid out strict directives that each person was to gather enough for one day only, barring his double provision before each Sabbath (see Ex 16:5). God provided supernaturally for the Hebrews, but the people had the responsibility whether or not to receive his provision.

It is the same for us today. This time Jesus is the Bread of Life.

'Our forefathers ate the manna in the desert; as it is written: "He gave them bread from heaven to eat." '...Jesus said to them, 'I tell you the truth, it is not Moses who has given you the bread from heaven, but it is my Father who gives you the true bread from heaven. For the bread of God is he who comes down from heaven and gives life to the world...I am the bread of life. *He who comes to me* will never go hungry, and *he who believes in me* will never be thirsty' (Jn 6:31–33,35, italics mine).

Just like the manna, Jesus provides all the nutrients and goodness we need to continue the walk through our own particular desert. Jesus is available to us on a daily basis, should we choose to avail ourselves of this provision. If we fail to accept that responsibility, we will go hungry and look back to Egypt—our past lesbian life—for subsistence.

Jesus is not an instant food experience like a McDonald's—he offers more satisfying and nutritious sustenance which shapes and fortifies a person.

Memories and murmurings

The Israelites' memories were not only short, but also distorted. Foreigners—possibly Egyptians or Ethiopians—who had travelled with the Hebrews, soon began moaning. They forgot the bad aspects of Egypt, the cruelty and the hardship, but focused its carnal pleasure.

'If only we had meat to eat! We remember the fish we ate in Egypt at no cost—also the cucumbers, melons, leeks, onions and garlic. But now we have lost our appetite; we never see anything but this manna!' (Num 11:4–6).

Did the Israelites rebuke these foreigners for snubbing God's provision of the manna? Not at all. Scripture tells us that every man wept at his own tent door (see Num 11:10). Obviously self-pity was the order of the day.

There will always be people who will question the validity of change from lesbianism and your personal growth. Your friends will be selective in their memories, and the media in their accounts of the homosexual lifestyle. They will enhance the good and ignore the bad.

When we feel lonely it is easy to console ourselves with memories. This does not breed comfort, but dissatisfaction. We are easily drawn down memory lane, reliving the past and destroying the present healing in our lives. We must combat this temptation and, instead, use our lonely feelings as an offering to God, a springboard into greater intimacy with him.

Practical help in overcoming loneliness

Without an ongoing relationship with the Lord, no amount of practical help will curb one's loneliness. However, if that relationship is developing well and you are still engulfed by 'terminal loneliness', then there are other areas to address.

For a number of months, Tessa had been so consumed by developing intimacy with Jesus that little else seemed to bother her. But lately she was becoming increasingly dissatisfied with her life.

'Jeanette, does it sound heretical to say that God's not enough for me?' Tessa asked in her usual subtle manner.

'Can you elaborate just a little?' I asked non-committedly.

'My relationship with God is great, better than it's ever been. But recently I've found myself wanting more. You know—someone to laugh with, to touch, someone who's human! I have some friends but they just aren't cutting it. I want more than they can offer me. I guess I'm feeling kind of lonely. I'm scared to push myself too much in case I fall into another dependent relationship. What can I do?'

I thought for a moment. 'Tessa, I doubt if there is one person on earth who doesn't feel like you do at some point in their lives. God does understand your needs. The first part of Psalm 68:6 says: "God sets the lonely in families, he leads forth the prisoners with singing."

'Your desire for intimate fellowship is a God-given desire. Let's go over a few ways you can prepare yourself for developing godly and intimate friendships.'

'Great!' Tessa enthusiastically grabbed for her notebook and pen.

Self-evaluation

Once Tessa had settled down, I continued. 'The first step is to assess yourself. What do you really want? Is it a more casual, social contact or a more deep, familiar contact? When we are products of dependent relationships, we often want immediate intimacy and are dissatisfied with anything less. I know of one woman who truly believed that she had no friends. Why? Because neither she nor they had this overwhelming need to live in each others pockets. Without this emotional rush, she incorrectly concluded that the relationships were of little depth.'

'So, the first question is to know what I want?' asked Tessa, scribbling furiously.

'Exactly. And that isn't as cut and dried as it sounds. We don't always know what we want or what we need! However, if it is social contact you desire, then that can be somewhat satisfied by committing yourself to the singles group in your church, if you have one. There are often women's meetings that you can also visit. If there are mid-week Bible studies, then you can attend one of those regularly.'

Tessa looked up from her notes. 'It's kind of scary to go to these groups.'

'That's true,' I agreed. 'I still find myself shying away from true commitment to groups. But the reality is that intimacy develops out of social friendships. We'll talk about building friendships later. Suffice it to say that we need to take the plunge into society even when we feel out of place.'

'What else do I have to do?'

'There is a real hiatus between coming out of lesbianism and walking into healthy same-sex friendships. During this period, the temptation to return to our sin is perhaps at its strongest. We feel abandoned between two camps— one godly, and the other sinful—and without the friendship of either party. At this point we need to be spiritually alert and ready for war. Satan and the world would have us believe that loneliness is our lot in life. But 2 Corinthians 10:5 states: "We demolish arguments and every pretension that sets itself up against the knowledge of God, and we take captive every thought to make it obedient to Christ."

'This means that we can offset accusations or faulty beliefs by measuring them against what we know of God's character, and through what is written in the word.'

After writing down the Scripture reference, Tessa looked up. 'Is there a concrete step I can do right now?'

'Yes,' I replied. 'You can be accountable for your time.'

Tessa looked confused. 'How do you mean?'

'Over the next week, write down all your activities other than your job, and the amount of time you spend at each one. At the end of the week, categorise those areas in the following way.' I gave her a worksheet to fill in over the next seven days.

I.   How much time do you spend alone?
II.   How much time do you spend in building your faith?
      A. alone
      B. with others
III. How much time do you spend daydreaming or being self-preoccupied?
IV.   How much time do you spend in habitual, unproduc-

tive activities (ie, always turning on the TV as soon as you get home from work)?

V.   How much time do you spend forging relationships (ie, actively speaking to three new people at church each Sunday)?

Tessa seemed excited at this practical step. 'Then what do I do with the information?' she asked.

'Your actions will obviously depend on the results of your survey,' I answered. 'But it will help you know your strong and weak areas. Then you can gradually decrease your time alone or habitually watching television, and increase your time with others. Whatever you feel is necessary.'

'Great!' cried Tessa excitedly. 'I'll start tomorrow. Then I want to know all about building friendships,' she yelled as she bounded through the doorway.

For further study

1. *Loneliness* by Elisabeth Elliot (Oliver-Nelson: USA, 1988) (UK edition: Kingsway Publications, 1990).
2. *Facing Loneliness: The Starting Point of a New Journey* by Oswald Sanders (Highland Books, 1988).
3. *Happiness is a Choice: A Manual of the Symptoms, Causes, and Cures of Depression* by Frank B Minirth and Paul D Meier (Baker Book House: USA, 1978).
4. *Why Be Lonely? A Guide to Meaningful Relationships* by W Leslie Carter, Paul D Meier and Frank B Minirth (Baker Book House: USA, 1982).

For your own evaluation

HOURS SPENT EACH DAY							
How much time do you spend:	**Mon**	**Tues**	**Wed**	**Thur**	**Fri**	**Sat**	**Sun**
1. Alone?							
2. In building your faith alone?							
3. In building your faith with others?							
4. Daydreaming or being self-preoccupied?							
5. In habitual, unproductive activities?							
6. Forging relationships?							
TOTAL							

Adapted from Craig Ellison *Loneliness: The Search for Intimacy* (Christian Herald Books, 1980).

CHAPTER TEN

DEVELOPING HEALTHY SAME-SEX FRIENDSHIPS

Homosexuality is a relational problem. Interference in the bonding/identification process with the mother and other female role models lies at the root of a lesbian's struggle. Since faulty same-sex relationships constitute the core of the problem, healthy same-sex relationships are a vital factor in the healing process. To leave lesbianism behind and to avoid further dependency, it is essential to develop such friendships.

Isolation—a by-product of dependency

Ignoring the rest of the world is easy when we are enmeshed in dependent relationships. Other friendships fade into the background as we spend the majority of our waking hours engrossed in one particular person. Walking away from the bondage of dependency requires not only a time of 'emotional celibacy', but also a walk toward healthy same-sex friendships.

We seldom feel like taking this step. Our tendency is to withdraw and remain isolated from society. We are engrossed with thoughts such as, *If I can't have Jane then I don't want anyone; no one can replace Jane.* This withdrawal from the rest of humanity proves detrimental to our health. We focus on our deep sense of loss which, in turn, increases our feeling of loneliness. When the pain becomes unbearable, we emerge from our self-imposed isolation and pounce on the nearest person, internally demanding that they meet all our needs.

Therefore, we must learn to deny ourselves the option of withdrawal, and we must seek God's way of filling that gaping hole left by a past dependency. Where we once sought completion through one woman, we must now seek fellowship through a group of people. As we saw in chapter 9, Sheila found that opening herself to a broader range of friendships helped offset the sense of loss she was experiencing.

For some ex-lesbians, dependency upon another has not been an issue for a number of years. This is not necessarily because of healing; it may result from self-imposed isolation. They have bound themselves in emotional barbed wire and hung up a sign saying, 'Keep Out'. Fear of dependency prevents healthy intimacy from ever taking place.

God's call to relationships

As we noted in chapter 7, Susan recognised the need to relinquish her own itinerary for the future, and allow God to move freely in her thoughts, emotions and subsequent actions. Susan shared with me during counselling that the years of self-sufficiency were not lying down without a struggle.

One particular afternoon, Susan was especially agitated. Although our counselling sessions had been progressing well, Susan had expressed increasing discomfort whenever the subject of vulnerability arose. Deciding that a change of venue could prove beneficial, I seized my Bible and personal notes on the subject and suggested a drive to the nearby beach.

We ambled along the water's edge. The incessant pounding of the Pacific surf and the screeching of the gulls overhead were the only sounds to break our silent stroll. Wisdom gained from past experience told me not to hurry Susan. She found it difficult to share her thoughts and feelings.

Susan finally spoke. 'I'm in a dilemma.' She paused. 'I sense God is wanting me to venture out into the world of relationships. First, I don't want to, and second, I don't know how. Jeanette, you appear to have a number of close friends. How did you do it?'

Now it was my turn to be silent. It had not been that long since I was in a situation similar to Susan's. We sat down on the warm sand. 'Susan, it took a long while to accept the fact that God wanted me to have deep relationships. In the past, my friendships always had an air of superficiality about them. I had so many self-protective walls that true intimacy with another was impossible. Of course, there were some people who managed to scale a few of the walls and get close. But, generally speaking, I isolated myself from others.

'Then God began to speak to me through sermons, books and other people. Everything I listened to, read or spoke about had to do with relationships. Before long I could sense my anger rising. I told God that I didn't want or need other people.'

'That's just how I feel,' interrupted Susan. 'I guess I believe that the cost of relating is just too high.'

I looked at her. 'In what way?' I asked.

Fear of vulnerability

Susan let the grains of sand sift through her fingers. 'I know that if I am to become a real friend to someone, I'm going to have to be vulnerable. But that is contrary to anything I have ever believed in or acted upon in the past.'

'What does being vulnerable mean to you?'

'It means that I open myself up to being used, possibly even abused, by others. It means that I'm out of control, because if I share, people could use the information against me. People would also know those nasty areas that only God and I know at present. They would find out my motivation behind some of my actions, shameful motivations that would embarrass me. Finally, admitting my true self to another person might prevent my plans from being realised. They may conclude that I am not the right person for a job or a ministry position.'

Susan had obviously given this some thought! She had also expressed some legitimate fears.

God has an uncanny knack of reminding me of my past. I laughed. 'Susan,' I said, 'talking with you is like hearing myself! You have a certain amount of fear regarding the issue of vulnerability, and I understand that. But you also have to deal with the issue of pride. Pride separates us from people and condemns us to a life of isolation. We think that it's a weakness to have faults and problems, rather than recognising them as an inherent part of our makeup. Silence about our true self breeds fear, but confession of our weaknesses opens up channels of communication with other people.'

'But people will hurt me,' blurted out Susan, her eyes welling up with tears. 'I feel trapped. Underneath all my statements to the contrary, I do want friends—I really do. But it's safer for me to remain where I am. This way no one will reject me.'

Lightly touching Susan on the arm, I tried to pacify her. 'This is where we need to exercise discernment. We aren't meant to share deeply with everyone. Indiscriminate sharing really opens a person up to rejection. Some people are simply not able to cope with other people's problems. And that's okay. We are to ask God to give us the names of those who *are* able to listen and help. Letting God choose the right people minimises the possibility of rejection.

'Now, Susan, I want you to consider Jesus for just one moment.'

Jesus—an example of openness

I pulled out my notes and continued. 'In his book, *The Father Heart of God*, Floyd McClung describes Jesus' life in this way.'

> His very birth was questioned, and his mother's reputation was slandered. He was born in poverty. His race was ostracised and his home town ridiculed. His father died when he was young and in his latter years Jesus travelled the streets and cities homeless. He was misunderstood in his ministry, and abandoned in death.[8]

'Jesus had every reason to emotionally withdraw from people.' I met Susan's gaze. 'His life was a series of hurtful incidents, each one giving reason enough to isolate himself from society. But his reaction was the opposite to many of our responses to a painful past. He remained vulnerable to people, and He stayed open in his interactions with others.' I paused, allowing Susan to contemplate the reality of Jesus' life.

'Let me give you a few examples to consider,' I continued. 'Take his relationship with Judas Iscariot. From the onset, Jesus knew that Judas would ultimately betray him. Yet we see Judas included as one of the twelve disciples. Jesus shared his life intimately with someone who would definitely harm him.'

Susan smiled briefly. 'And I worry about those who might hurt me!'

Taking my tattered Bible from my pocket, I turned to John 11:32–36 where Jesus openly wept at the death of his friend, Lazarus. After reading the passage silently together, I continued leafing through the pages.

'Consider his profound love for the citizens of Jerusalem.'

> As he approached Jerusalem and saw the city, he wept over it and said, 'If you, even you, had only known on this day what would bring you peace—but now it is hidden from your eyes' (Lk 19:41–42).

'He knew that in a matter of days, his own people would reject and kill him. However, Christ's reaction was not to walk away from the pain, but to walk toward it. Like it says in the gospels, he set his face like a flint toward Jerusalem, where he would undergo his final days.'

God was beginning to minister to me as well as to Susan. I continued. 'Jesus watched his closest friends— Peter, James and John—abandon him at Gethsemane. But even that did not cause him to shut people out or to revoke his love for them. Although he gained little help from them, Jesus did receive the assistance of an angel. Susan, in order to receive anything, we have to recognise our need. Jesus knew that he needed relief, and he welcomed his Father's provision: "An angel from heaven appeared to him and strengthened him" (Lk 22:43).

'That night Peter followed Jesus at a distance. He witnessed Christ's suffering, and was later able to write about it.' Glancing back at my notes, I shared a passage from the Phillips New Testament.

> For Christ suffered for you and left you a personal example, so that you might follow in His footsteps. He was guilty of no sin nor of the slightest prevarication. Yet when He was insulted He offered no insult in return. When He suffered He made no threats of revenge. He simply committed His cause to the One who judges fairly (1 Pet 2:21–23, PHILLIPS).

'But, Jeanette, that makes it sound so easy!' moaned Susan. ' *"He simply committed His cause."* ' She pondered that thought for a moment. 'I guess I'm too concerned with the immediate repercussions of making myself vulnerable.'

'You could be right,' I agreed. 'Listen to this verse I have from Hebrews.'

Keep your eyes on Jesus, our leader and instructor. He was willing to die a shameful death on the cross *because of the joy he knew would be his afterwards*; and now he sits in the place of honour by the throne of God (Heb 12:2, TLB, italics mine).

I tucked my notes into my Bible. 'In the same way, we have to see this whole issue of vulnerability as an opportunity to place our trust in God. God's provision for us is not only through a relationship with him, but also through fellowship with others. Furthermore, Jesus could not present himself as invulnerable and impervious to pain because he was a man who loved. And true love lays itself open to hurt.'

Both of us became lost in our own thoughts as we walked back along the beach. I weighed my own fear of vulnerability against the pleasure of true companionship I had received when I opened myself up to others. 'Help me to be more open to you, Jesus, and to your ways,' I had prayed, 'so that I may experience all that you have to offer me.'

Unlike Susan, Tessa did not have such a deep-rooted fear of vulnerability. If anything, her problem was one of over-enthusiasm when it came to making friends!

Making a plan of action

The next day, as my car turned into the driveway, I noticed Tessa's familiar red jacket flung on the steps of the office. I groaned. It was 9am, and I was not sure if I was ready for another of Tessa's onslaughts quite so early in the morning! I had hardly locked the car door when she leaped next to me with unsuppressed fervour, exclaiming, 'I'm ready to relate!'

I quickly glanced heavenward. *Why me, Lord?* I thought as I stumbled towards the door. However, it was hard not to get caught up in Tessa's excitement as she shared her completed activity chart with me. She had faithfully kept track of all her non-working hours, and had already implemented some changes in her life.

'I've stopped turning the TV on at random. I found that I relied on its noise to prevent me from getting in touch with my thoughts. Now I'm much more conscious of what I am feeling at any given moment. I've also committed myself to attend the singles' meetings every week, and go to Bible study regularly.'

'That's great, Tess,' I smiled warmly. 'Now I want to explain to you the different levels of friendship you can expect.'

Defining your friendships

Once settled in the office, I proceeded to show her my friendship diagram. (See Diagram 1)[9]

'The outer circle represents your acquaintances,' I said. 'This circle will consist of the greatest number of people. Your expectations of them and commitment to them will be low.'

Tessa interjected, 'What kind of people are they?'

'Some of them will be people you work with, people at church, or, perhaps, those you meet at places like the health club. You will be on speaking terms with them, but it's rare that either of you share anything of major significance about yourself. The conversation will be pretty superficial and non-demanding.

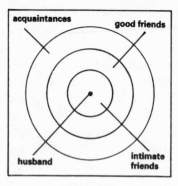

Diagram 1

I pointed to the diagram again. 'The middle circle is for those whom you consider to be good friends. These may be people in your Bible study, and a few people in the singles' group. Ultimately, I guess you can expect to build up a group of about ten good friends.'

Tessa appeared downcast. 'Why so few?'

'Tessa, successful relationships require dedication and hard work. Friendships are an investment which take time to mature. We don't have the capacity to be deep and meaningful with everyone, even if we wanted to!'

Somewhat encouraged, Tessa continued, 'So what makes good friends so different from acquaintances?'

'There has to be a trust factor in these relationships because a person is sharing some part of themselves. And because vulnerability opens us up to the possibility of getting hurt, we share with discretion. With a good friend we explore comfortable boundaries of sharing, recognising that each is an individual with definite likes and dislikes. Unlike emotionally dependent relationships, where boundaries between two people are cloudy or non-existent, healthy relating ensures that there is a continual separation between the two parties.'

Tessa planted her elbows firmly on the desk, cradling

her head in her hands. 'I think I understand, Jeanette. But can you give me an example of exploring comfortable boundaries?'

Sucking the end of my pen, I leant back in my chair and thought. 'It would be inappropriate for me to launch into a conversation about my deepest feelings with someone I barely knew.'

'I did with you,' Tessa interjected.

'That's different, Tess. We are counselling together and not attempting to form a friendship on a peer level. If my purpose is to develop a friendship, I should begin to talk about general subjects, like the possibility of war in the Middle East.'

Contorting her face, Tessa exclaimed, 'Yuck, couldn't you find something easier to talk about?'

Sometimes it was nearly impossible to keep control of these sessions with Tessa. 'Just listen,' I said. 'By addressing a general subject, I am able to share my opinions without disclosing too much about myself. Therefore, my feelings won't be hurt if she disagrees. If our relationship progresses well and both of us choose to pursue it further, subsequent conversations could cover areas that disclose more about each of us. This requires greater vulnerability. However, I can still tread carefully and only express areas that are irrefutable, such as my feelings. These cannot be right or wrong, they are merely telling this friend about me.'

Tessa nodded. 'So, it's okay to disagree about certain areas and still remain friends. You respect each other's opinions without trying to change them.'

'Yes.' Redirecting our focus back to the diagram, I continued. 'The final circle is for intimate friends. There is not a great difference between good friends and intimate friends. But an intimate friend is definitely at a peer level with you. Here you have an equality in the sharing and receiving of your thoughts, ideas and feelings. Compatibility and a deep level of trust are foundational to such friendships. Because of the commitment factor involved, you will only have the capacity to have three or four people in this circle.'

'Would you consider Carol to be one of your intimate friends?' asked Tessa.

'Yes, she fulfils all the criteria I've just mentioned. Not only do we share our feelings, we go even further with our friendship. I share my attitudes—decisions I've made about my life—with her. Attitudes are more personal than opinions. Again, intimacy requires greater vulnerability because misunderstanding and hurt can occur when our attitudes are questioned. I need to know that she is not intentionally wanting to hurt me if she disagrees.'

Tessa thought about the definitions for a while before asking another question. 'Jeanette, what happens to these circles if I get married?'

'Good question. The centre dot is for your husband. God tells us that in marriage the two become one. That is the ultimate earthly intimacy we can achieve.'

Tessa studied the diagram for a minute. 'What else do I need to know?' she asked.

Holding friendships lightly—not tightly

'Tessa, a lot of what you learn about friendships will only come through practice. But I do want to encourage you to hold relationships lightly on the palm of your hand. When we are bound up in dependency, there is a temptation to hold the friendship tightly in our fist for fear of losing it. The plan backfires because we find that our grip chokes the relationship. Then God has to pry open our fingers to release the other person from our grasp.'

Tessa winced. 'Is that what makes the breaking-free process so painful?'

'Yes,' I agreed. 'So much of us wants to hold on to what

we have. Our flesh is a formidable foe! But if relationships lie on an open palm, it means that God can freely move people at his will. You see, Tessa, relationships are living things and no two are the same. They are always changing. Take a look at this other diagram.' I pulled out the pie chart. (See Diagram 2.)

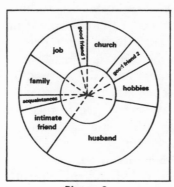

Diagram 2

'Each person is a segment of the pie,' I explained, 'but Jesus is the centre of the pie. He is the one who holds all the other pieces together. Jesus has the freedom to shift the boundaries and move people in and out of our lives according to our needs and his plan for us.'

Tessa slumped before my eyes. 'I don't think I can do this, Jeanette. I just know I'm going to mess up. It's too difficult.'

I smiled with compassion. 'It *is* hard, Tess, and you *are* going to make mistakes. It would be unrealistic to expect yourself to float through this process without problems. But there are some things that you can do which will help you in this process of healthy relating.' It was time for me to talk about honesty and accountability.

A flicker of hope returned to Tessa's eyes.

Honesty and accountability

'In the past,' I continued, 'many of us have entered into clandestine relationships, hidden behind half truths, and used deceit to continue in our lesbian sin. But for healing to occur, we need to commit ourselves to honesty in our relationships. Honesty requires humility.

'There are two common fears that prevent honest confession. First, we fear losing everything familiar to us. Second, we're afraid of living without one special person in our life. Although those are understandable fears, the Bible is clear on the benefits of disclosure.'

'Therefore confess your sins to each other and pray for each other *so that you may be healed*' (Jas 5:16, italics mine).

'Tessa, we may be tempted to focus on the immediate pain of giving up something or someone to the detriment of the long-term healing.'

'What are the benefits of honesty?' quizzed Tessa.

'Fellowship with God and subsequently with others.' I read her 1 John 1:6-7, which states: 'If we claim to have fellowship with him yet walk in the darkness, we lie and do not live by the truth. But if we walk in the light, as he is in the light, we have fellowship with one another, and the blood of Jesus, his Son, purifies us from all sin.'

Tessa looked puzzled about something. 'Jeanette, in the Bible study this week, someone mentioned the word *accountable*. Everyone nodded their head as though they understood what he was talking about. I didn't, but I was too embarrassed to ask him to explain. What is accountability?'

Immediately, my thoughts flashed back in time. *What an important concept to understand and implement. If only I had known about it earlier, perhaps*—but my thoughts were suddenly interrupted by Tessa.

'Jeanette, can you explain it to me?'

I quickly pulled myself together. 'Accountability means talking *before* we commit an act of sin—talking to someone *while* we are tempted, not after the sin has taken place. Accountability brings change because it helps break the sin cycle. For instance, if I'm struggling with emotional dependency and I am prone to calling this woman as soon as I return home after work, I need to find a way to interrupt the behavioural pattern. Tessa, if this were your dilemma, can you think of practical ways you could interrupt this particular problem?'

She looked out of the window, deep in thought. 'Perhaps I can change my method of transport and arrive home at a different time. Or I could make arrangements to visit a friend. I could choose to make that hour my quiet time with God, maybe stay out of the house and, therefore, away from the phone.'

'That's great planning, Tess.'

She beamed.

'As the cycle of sin is broken,' I continued, 'we are able to discern what we are truly feeling at the time of temptation. When we deny ourselves the quick emotional fix another person offers, we allow God to minister to our real needs.

'However I choose to overcome this temptation, it is equally important to make my weaknesses known to others. That's another important part of accountability. It gives them permission to question my after-work activities—in depth, if necessary. When we choose to combat sin areas, we will be tempted to lie, play games and continue to put ourselves in compromising situations. Making ourselves accountable to spiritually mature people within the church helps us out of our sin.'

Tessa's forehead furrowed. 'But isn't my sin between me and God? Why can't I just confess it to him, or be accountable only to him? Why do other people have to know?'

I smiled, sensing that Tessa had a problem with relinquishing control in this area. 'Tessa, God is the easiest person to ignore. Because he is intangible, we excuse ourselves far too readily. We need humility and vulnerability to ensure victory over sin. Frank Worthen, director of Exodus Manila, says, "The height of my victory is equal to the depth of my submission." The more accountable we make ourselves to others, the greater our possibilities for complete healing. Again, we ask God to direct us to the right people with whom we can be accountable. They need not be the same people to whom we are vulnerable, because the two concepts are not synonymous with each other.'

Tessa had been given enough information for one day. I could see that her desire to remain autonomous in her healing was battling against the need for accountability in her life. During our next counselling session I would cover other areas in walking out of lesbianism and toward the promised land.

The benefits of a support system

Later, as I thought about my talk with Tessa, I realised that developing a support system works in tandem with creating accountability in our lives. A support network consists of people from a variety of backgrounds who empathise with your struggle. They are able to give you a different perspective than your own.

One particular incident in my life proved the importance of having such a system. I had been actively seeking healing for two years. By that time, I had established a check list of characteristics I found attractive in a woman. It was not hard to do. By listing all my past lovers and dependencies, I was able to discern a definite pattern to my unhealthy attractions. Although no two women looked the same, they all exhibited two or more of the following characteristics: a gentle spirit, a hint of vulnerability, a caring attitude, softness, competence and athleticism.

I lined this information up against my own view of self. With a few exceptions, such as athletic ability, they were areas in which I felt personally inadequate. I wanted what they had.

In counselling, we call this 'cannibal compulsion'. Leanne Payne addresses this subject of cannibal compulsion in her book, *The Broken Image*.[10] She shared with a counsellee, Matthew, the following:

> I then told him what a missionary once told me: 'Cannibals eat only those they admire, and they eat them to get their traits.' What was happening to Matthew was very clear: he was looking at the other young man and loving a lost part of himself, a part that he could not recognise and accept.

Knowing this information took the mystery out of any subsequent attractions I experienced. In fact, it became rather boring to realise that these attractions could be so easily explained. Once the mystery had been solved, and I was not face to face with the 'woman of my dreams', the attraction tended to take a back seat in my life. Further healing took place as I began to embrace and not deny, those attributes in me.

However, about a year after I had created this list, I was shaken, rather abruptly, out of my boredom. The incident occurred at a time when I was exploring relationships with 'straight' women. I was aghast at my attraction to one particular woman and quickly examined my motives for desiring her friendship. All seemed above board. Although she exhibited a couple of my 'red flag' characteristics, I didn't believe I was seeking a dependent or physical relationship. But nagging voices inside kept telling me that attraction to *any* woman was wrong, and this friendship was to be avoided, not pursued.

Very confused by the whole incident, I questioned a woman in my support network about my dilemma. This friend was an 'ever-straight', someone who had never struggled with homosexuality.

She laughed at my problem. 'Why would you want to be friends if you weren't attracted to a person?' she asked incredulously. 'Attraction isn't necessarily sexual. I'm attracted to all of my girlfriends. There's nothing strange about that.'

What a relief! By bouncing my fears off someone else, I was able to arrive at a reasonable conclusion. I struck up a casual friendship with the 'problem' woman. However, because of my dependent background, I still made myself accountable regarding my feelings and attention towards my new-found friend.

Motivation

If we have come to terms with being honest with God and ourselves, we are more able to discern our motivations in establishing friendships. We must ask ourselves searching questions:

1. What are the limits of my friendship? Do I use people, or do I lay down my life for them? How much do I know of sacrificial love?
2. What is my impact on others? Am I an agent for change in my friend's life? Is she more of a disciple because of me?
3. Am I open in our friendship? Do I present myself as being 'all together' in her company, or do I readily admit my faults?
4. Do I initiate love and service? Or do I wait for others to earn my approval or to reach out to me?
5. Do I choose people as my friends because of my needs or out of common interests we have?
6. How am I helping my friend realise her potential in any or every area of life? Is she fruitful because of me?[11]

In his book, *The Four Loves*[12], C S Lewis pictures good friends as standing shoulder to shoulder, side by side, focusing on a common interest. He contrasts that posture to one of lovers standing face to face, engrossed in each other.

When we are products of dependent relationships, we are prone to turn inward—face to face—absorbed in each other and separated from anything or anyone else.

For most of my life, my friendships have assumed the face-to-face posture. Although we had mutual hobbies and interests—and that included Christianity—our primary focus was on each other. This tight group of two did not welcome intruders who would block our view of each other. In our minds, the circle was complete.

However, godly friendships are healthy friendships—and I needed to pursue them. In order to do this, I had to reposition myself and allow people to enter and exit the scene without clutching on to them.

I was able to learn more about developing healthy same-sex relationships by observing the friendships maintained by 'straight' women in the church body. However, this observation also highlighted another area that required God's touch—my inability to accept myself as a woman, and to embrace all that I understood to be inherently feminine.

For further study

1. *The Father Heart of God* by Floyd McClung (Kingsway Publications: UK, 1985) (US edition: Harvest House, 1985).

2. *Concentric Circles of Concern* by Oscar Thompson (Broadman Press: USA, 1981).

3. *The Broken Image: Restoring Personal Wholeness Through Healing Prayer* by Leanne Payne (Crossway Books: 1981) (UK edition: Kingsway Publications, 1988).

4. *Quality Friendship: The Risks and Rewards* by Gary Inrig (Moody Press: USA, 1981).
5. *The Four Loves* by C S Lewis (Harcourt Brace Jovanovich: USA, 1960) (UK edition: Fontana, 1963).

CHAPTER ELEVEN

I AM WOMAN!

Although I grew up female by physical design, I grew up confused about my sexuality. Feeling more like some 'third sex' than male or female, I stumbled my way through life, paving my own path of gender identity, unsure of my direction or purpose. For years I was a gender-identity itinerant, migrating somewhere between the masculine, feminine and neuter.

This meandering did not immediately cease upon my conversion. But a major turning point came when I was two years old in the Lord.

'Jeanette, stand in front of the mirror every morning and thank God that he's made you a woman.' This challenge came from a teacher at the Bible School I attended as a young Christian.

What a ridiculous task! I thought, but reluctantly agreed.

The next morning I got up and struggled to look at myself in the mirror. Try as I would, I could not acknowledge myself as truly female.

Day after day I persevered. For the first week I fought merely to hold my gaze at the mirror, unable to utter a word. After about ten days, I was able to look at myself

177

full face. But when it came to saying anything, I could not speak. I just cried, too frightened to acknowledge who I was.

Only after several weeks could I stand in front of the mirror and say, 'Thank you, Father, for making me a woman.' No sentence has ever been as hard to say as that one. Yet it was a key step for me to take in the process of changing my gender identification. By accepting my God-given physical gender, I was bringing my thoughts into alignment with God.

Growing up, I had felt so out of place as a woman, it was very tempting to entertain thoughts that God some-how made a mistake. Coming into agreement with God, however, meant acknowledging that he not only knew me but approved of me. He chose me to be a woman. In fact, he saw me as being completely female, irrespective of my own thoughts on the matter. God knew what he was doing! 'Before I formed you in the womb I knew you, before you were born I set you apart' (Jer 1:5).

No longer would I refer to myself as a Christian person, as I had for the past several years. From now on, out of obedience to God, I would call myself a Christian *woman*.

Although my head accepted the fact that I was a woman, unfortunately, my heart was seemingly untouched by this knowledge.

A new name—a new identity

A further breakthrough came two years after the incident with the mirror. At a women's retreat, God exposed the false labels behind which many women had been hiding and sovereignly changed the way they viewed themselves.

One woman shared how God had changed her 'name' from Stubborn to Persevering One. Another spoke of her name change from Abused to Nurturer.

'What about me, God?' I asked desperately. 'What new name do you have for me?'

'You have believed a lie,' he revealed. 'But I am going to change your name. From now on you will know yourself as *Woman*.'

His words pierced me. Woman! The very name proclaimed my real gender identity. Years of confusion and anguish fell away as I embraced that elusive identity. What had once appeared so intangible, now became a heart reality to me. God had touched me at the very centre of my being.

At this point I did not know the ramifications of this heart knowledge. Then I looked around at the sea of female faces at the retreat. Something had changed. I no longer stood apart. For the first time in my life, these women seemed accessible to me—sisters in the Lord. It was an amazing feat on God's part! Never before had I felt any sense of unity with other women. That perceived chasm between myself and 'real' women had been one crucial factor in my entering an active lesbian existence.

What's in a name? Plenty!

Two years later, Lisa, a 'straight' friend of mine, shared with me how important that retreat had been to her. 'God revealed to me some of the names I'd laboured under for so long,' Lisa told me. 'Names like Worthless, Failure and Angry. He showed me that Satan had used each of these names as a weapon to keep me from recognising my true worth in Christ.'

I listened intently. 'What else did God say?'

'He showed me that the names I operated under were only one side of a coin. The flip side reflected the names God had given me—my true names. But, because of our fallen state, Satan has managed to twist what is God-given and present us with a distorted view of self. Unfortunately, most of us agree with Satan in his distortion.'

I nodded. 'But how do we walk out of this predicament?'

'God changes our name when we line up our view of self with his thinking and design for us.'

'It all fits into place,' I exclaimed. 'When I chose to view myself as a woman four years ago, even though I didn't feel like one, I basically tossed the coin into the air. I'm really glad it's now facing head up! Not only do I know my true name, I'm now able to embrace all that it entails. What were your God-given names?'

Lisa smiled, obviously delighted with her real identity. My true names are 'Valued Child, Conqueror and Prayer Warrior.'

Jesus—the epitome of balance

Shortly after the women's retreat, God began leading me to Scriptures which illustrated His masculine and feminine characteristics. (Some of those Scriptures are recorded in chapter 3.) He assured me that he was not only powerful and creative—the masculine—but that he was also nurturing and responsive to me—the feminine. Then I found a thought-provoking section in Leanne Payne's book, *Crisis in Masculinity*.

> Our Creator, holding all that is true and real within himself, reflects both the masculine and the feminine, *and so do we*. The more nearly we function in his image, the more nearly we reflect both the masculine and the feminine in their proper balance [italics mine].[13]

Now conscious of this aspect of God's character, I found him encouraging me to see Jesus as a role model of balanced masculinity and femininity. This was difficult for me to do at first. Like most women struggling to leave the lesbian life, I found it hard to fully embrace Jesus as my example. 'But he's a man!' we argue, convincing ourselves that he could not possibly understand our female predicaments. However, the Bible is clear: Jesus empathises with all our trials: 'This high priest of ours understands our weaknesses, since he had the same temptations we do, though he never once gave way to them and sinned' (Heb 4:15, TLB).

I started exploring the gospels. As I studied, I discovered the feminine and masculine traits in the character of Jesus. The feminine side of Jesus as a human is found in his ability to *listen* to His Father, and to *respond* to the Father's leading. Listening preceded action. 'I do nothing on my own but speak just what the Father has taught me. The one who sent me is with me; he has not left me alone, for I always do what pleases him' (Jn 8:28–29).

Similarly, Jesus *received* the sins of the world at his crucifixion, and Jesus *yielded* up his spirit at his death. Both of these actions are inherently feminine in their origin.

Regarding the masculine aspect of Jesus, he is the epitome of authority in all his actions. Jesus was decisive and assertive. He challenged people's thinking on any given subject (see Jn 4, the Samaritan woman at the well). Jesus became openly angry when he saw God's righteous standards being violated (see Jn 2:12–17, the cleansing of the temple).

The perfection of Christ includes the symmetry that exists between the feminine and the masculine. In this respect, Jesus is our perfect role model. He is the personification of Genesis 1:27: 'So God created man in his own image, in the image of God he created him; male and female he created them.'

Thus, we find the appropriate balance of masculine with feminine in Jesus—not in the world's caricatured female stereotypes. No, God does not necessarily want us to put curlers in our hair, don polyester-type dresses and just do housework, as I had wrongly assumed. Rather, he wants us to 'function in his image', as Leanne Payne put it so well.

Acceptance of our gender is only the first step toward functioning in God's image. Then we need to address other areas.

God knows you

In chapter 3, Susan renounced certain vows she had made regarding womanhood. Even though she felt confused, Susan, in faith, accepted God's view of her as a woman. Just as I had done, Susan had created a framework, through submission and obedience, in which God could fill in 'the missing pieces'—her feelings on the matter. Emotions eventually catch up with one's decision making.

Susan found Scripture memorisation very helpful to keep her thoughts on track. One of her favourite passages was Psalm 139:13–16.

> For you created my inmost being, you knit me together in my mother's womb. I praise you because I am fearfully and wonderfully made; your works are wonderful, I know that full well. My frame was not hidden from you when I was made in the secret place. When I was woven together in the depths of the earth, your eyes saw my unformed body. All the days ordained for me were written in your book before one of them came to be.

During one counselling session, Susan, in her customary curled up pose in my armchair, shared the following: 'Whenever I begin to question my identity, my worth, or God's care for me, I recall Psalm 139,' she said. 'Focusing on the truth that God planned my sexual make-up before my conception corrects any false notions I'm carrying around.'

I nodded in agreement.

Susan had come a long way over this past year, but the issue of the balance in her femininity continued to cause her pain. 'I know and have accepted the fact that God made me female,' she shared. 'Actually, for the most part, I'm beginning to enjoy being a woman. But I'm having a really hard time relinquishing my talents to God.' She sighed. 'I'm so afraid.'

Recognising that Susan was not going to continue without further prompting, I began to draw thoughts out of her. 'Can you identify this fear, Susan?'

'Yes, I'm afraid that if I recognise my strength and abilities are wrong, and I yield them to God, then I'll end up like some fluff ball!' She laughed at the confused expression which crossed my face. 'You know, blond, bubbly, but of no earthly use to anyone!'

'Susan, I detect a few misbeliefs,' I quickly interjected. 'What do you mean by recognising that your strengths and abilities are wrong?'

'Do you remember when I came to the realisation that I hid behind my ability? That I used it as a means of feeling okay about myself?'

'Yes.'

'Well, I've tried to get further than that point of realisation. I really want to fully submit to Jesus. But I'm afraid that God will take everything from me and I'll be left with nothing. Instead of being organised, efficient and dependable, I'll become disorganised, unproductive and unreliable. Jeanette, I'm not prepared to sacrifice that much of me.'

'Susan,' I answered, 'your abilities are not wrong in themselves. God gave you those abilities. The problem lies in how you've been using them. If they block your relationship with God, because they encourage self-sufficiency and independence, then God will want to deal with them—bring them under his Lordship—but not destroy them!

'The issue of pride is involved here,' I added. 'And God hates pride. I'm reminded of the Scripture about God opposing the proud, but giving grace to the humble [Jas 4:6]. Laying down our talents before God enables him to raise them up for his purpose and our blessing.'

Imbalance of the masculine and feminine

Susan was not unusual in thinking that to release her talents into God's hands was to lose some part of her self. Many women who were brought up with poor masculine role models hold similar views. In reaction to a negligent or unresponsive father, and coupled with an ambivalence or disdain toward her mother, the daughter assumes masculine functions. She rejects the feminine role model based on her view of her mother, and embraces all that is masculine. The woman focuses on what she can *do*, rather than on who she can *be*, and she places emphasis on self-reliance, perfectionism and competition. The woman becomes performance-oriented, and has a tendency to spend her energies on causes or 'rights' in which she believes. So often this is an unspoken cry for final recognition from her dad.

In my own past, the problem lay in the fact that I had been functioning in the 'masculine mode'. I had little problem with initiation. I was able to perform and accomplish many things. But I was woefully inept at receiving from anybody. 'Be still, and know that I am God' (Ps 46:10) was alien to me. Eventually, however, I realised that self-determination was detrimental to my Christian walk.

Because it required submission, listening to God did not come easily. He was calling me to yield to him when I wanted to assert myself. God desired that I get in touch with the feminine, responsive part of me. A frightening prospect.

What does he really want from me? I questioned, still not confident of God's motives.

The more I explored God and his purpose in my life, I was thrown into great confusion. He did not applaud my activity and achievements. Quite the contrary, God was encouraging me to stop my striving, to stop trying to earn his love, and to stop placing impossible expectations upon myself. God was challenging me to derive my worth from him!

I cried with frustration. 'But how, Father?' I pleaded. 'I don't know how to stop striving.' I did not know how to receive.

God challenged more than what I said or did. That I could have handled! He challenged *me*. Without my actions to hide behind, I felt defenceless, vulnerable and afraid. Larry Crabb addresses this issue in his book, *Inside Out*.

> When the businesslike woman sees her fear of being exploited or disdained if she offers what's really inside of her feminine heart, then she can better understand that her self-protection is a desperate attempt to hide her damaged womanhood. When she realises that beneath her defensive hardness is a woman, wounded and afraid, she may get an exciting glimpse of what it would mean to be fully female, a glimpse that will both terrify and entice her.[14]

God shone his light onto the dark recesses of my heart. He made me aware that there was more to me than action. There was emotion. There was a need to be cared for, nourished and protected. In my desire to reject all that was outwardly feminine, I had rejected my intuitive, responsive self in favour of my logical, assertive self. But as I caught a glimpse of God's design for me, I recognised my problem. I had been denying half of my true self—almost like a four-cylinder car limping along on two cylinders.

To walk in wholeness requires a more balanced

approach to life than we have been experiencing. It requires a compatibility between our masculine and feminine sides, which will produce harmony rather than discord.

Similarly, the masculine/feminine equilibrium has often been disturbed in a woman who has suffered abuse. Her thoughts encourage controlling and manipulative behaviour. *No one will ever hurt me again!* Thus, she keeps everyone at bay or controls them through seduction.

For whatever reason, many women adopt pseudo-masculinity as a form of self-protection. They reject all that is inherently feminine, and strive to obtain 'equality' with, or superiority over, men.

The destructiveness of this stance passes unnoticed because the world applauds our defense mechanisms. But the cost of this applause is high. By attaining 'equality' with men, we entomb our gentle, vulnerable and trusting qualities under a guise of toughness, independence and suspicion. We trust no one but ourselves. Our hard, protective layers smother our heart-cries to be cared for, held and loved.

The other end of the spectrum of imbalance manifests itself in women who derive their sense of identity and security from other people. Assuming the role of a child, these women rely on others to define and determine their lives. In this instance, they mistake passivity for femininity. This stance is just as unbalanced as the woman who strives for recognition through her actions. Continual grasping from other people obscures the woman's understanding of self. Without a firm base to fall back on, her relationships with others are precarious.

Just as all families lie somewhere on the dysfunction spectrum, so all women lie somewhere on the spectrum between acceptance and rejection of their gender and feminine identity.

On the one hand you may have encountered those

lesbians who personify all that is feminine and have no problems seeing themselves as such. On the other hand, you may have come across women who have denied their gender identity and femininity so much that, except for the obvious physiological differences, they could be mistaken for a male. But, the majority of those struggling with lesbianism fall in the murky middle ground.

Attitudes and beliefs about men vary, too, depending on our place on this curve. However, there is one predominant attitude I have encountered among nearly all lesbians: feeling superior to men.

Gender superiority

Even though I detached emotionally from my mother at an early age, women ran my life. I did have a father and two brothers, but I remember having very little interaction with them. From the age of five through to eighteen years, I had only one male teacher. In my mind, he was weak and ineffectual. Though he spoke eight languages, he was incapable of keeping order in a class of twenty-five lively nine-year-olds. My mother and I were equally contemptuous of him.

I did not have to consider men again for many years. Attending an all-girls' school where personal discipline and academic excellence were the order of the day, my already shaky femininity was further squelched. I had crushes on various teachers who positively dripped with femininity. Now I realise that I was attracted to qualities in them that I felt lacking in myself.

My true heroine was the vice-principal. She wore plaid skirts, steel rimmed glasses and strode around our ancient school building in well-polished brogues. An accomplished teacher of mathematics and car maintenance, Miss Daley scoffed at weak women and wimpy men. I adored her. She made me laugh and gave me a sense of purpose.

She encouraged me to be all that I could be—a 'self-made woman'. I gladly responded, and stepped joyfully onto the ladder of success.

Although I was very confused regarding my emerging homosexual feelings, I chose to place emphasis on my abilities in preference to dealing with my 'infirmities'. *I don't need a man*, I concluded. *There's nothing that they can do which I can't be equal to*.

These beliefs were reinforced during my three years at an all-women's physical education college. Although I encountered a smattering of men at this time, few of them ever challenged that deepening conviction I held. Yes, women were superior to men.

By the time I landed a teaching job at an all-girls' boarding school, my mind was long settled concerning this issue. Actively involved as a lesbian, there was no one to contest my persuasion regarding the ability of women, and I was proud of my superior status to men. Although I considered men useful in some instances, more often than not, I found them to be quite superfluous.

My deep beliefs on this subject did not change at my conversion. But God did not take long to address this issue in my life. At his prompting, I confessed my sinful belief in female superiority. I also asked God to show me why I held these thoughts, and asked him to help me understand the equality of both men and women in his eyes.

Over a period of time, godly, caring men entered my life. Initially I viewed them with suspicion, but their continued faithfulness and commitment to the Lord impressed me. Two pastors, although very different in their individual characters, truly personified that masculine/feminine balance exhibited by Jesus. One had the build of an American football player, the roar of a lion and the ability to cry like a child when moved by God or the plight of another. The other pastor was slight, quiet and unassuming. Yet he operated under the guidance of the Holy Spirit, and was not afraid to administer discipline when necessary. Both of them respected me as a person and as a woman. Both of them appreciated, though not always agreed with, my thoughts.

Their balanced approach accentuated the unstable ebb and flow of the masculine and feminine aspects of my own character. Surprisingly, instead of repulsing me, their masculine care and affirmation of me drew out a response that I had hitherto not known. I found myself beginning to respond to their caring, protective approach toward me. There was nothing sexual involved; it was the complementary aspect of the masculine and feminine responding to one another, almost like the opposite poles of a magnet.

A sleeping princess was beginning to awake!

This shook all my preconceived ideas of female superiority and male insignificance. *No woman is able to unleash this response in another female.* God used these pastors to show me the benefit of the opposite sex. He was showing me part of himself.

Trust—the key to embracing real femininity

Extricating oneself from anywhere on the spectrum of broken femininity is not easy. Many reasons, usually deep wounds, predisposed us to operating the way we do. But pain is an inherent part of our lives. It will never be eliminated this side of eternity. While reliance on self or other people may be our past pattern of living, Jeremiah 17:5–6 clearly states the consequences of this behaviour.

> Cursed is the [woman] who trusts in [others], who depends on flesh for [her] strength and whose heart turns away from the Lord. [She] will be like a bush in the wastelands; [she] will not see prosperity when it comes. [She] will dwell in the parched places of the desert, in a salt land where no one lives.

We cannot manufacture trust out of thin air simply

because the Bible encourages this attitude. Rather, obedience produces trust. Trust means responding to God's call even when we are unsure of what direction this will take us. Like a muscle, trust is built and strengthened with exercise. Trust in God enables us to enter his rest—to lean on his great power. Out of this rest, we are able to respond to God because strife has been replaced with security.

What are the benefits if I do trust God with every aspect of my life?

> But blessed is the [woman] who trusts in the Lord, whose confidence is in him. [She] will be like a tree planted by the water that sends out its roots by the stream. It does not fear when heat comes; its leaves are always green. It has no worries in a year of drought and never fails to bear fruit (Jer 17:7–8).

Trust in God has to be radical. Only action proves trust, and acting upon his promises brings change and blessing. God is not asking us to do anything new. Queen Esther faced the 'trust test' nearly three thousand years ago.

A Jewess, Esther was married to the King of Persia. Her uncle, Mordecai, sent a messenger to inform Queen Esther of a plot to eradicate the Jews from the Persian Empire. He challenged her to approach the king and intercede to spare her people.

There was a problem. Anyone who entered the king's inner court without being summoned would be summarily executed unless the king intervened. Esther was reluctant to act. Her husband had not summoned her to his court for a full thirty days. Fearing for her own life, she declined Mordecai's challenge.

Mordecai's response was clear:

> 'Do you think that you will escape there in the palace, when all other Jews are killed? If you keep quiet at a time like this, God will deliver the Jews from some other source, but you

and your relatives will die; what's more, who can say but that God has brought you into the palace for just such a time as this?' (Esther 4:13–14, TLB).

Here was the 'trust test' in its most basic form—place yourself fully into God's hands, even if it means death to self, and leave the outcome to him. In essence, Esther faced the same question we do as ex-lesbians: Do I side with the world in a feeble attempt to remain safe and uninvolved, or do I walk in my new, real identity as a daughter of God?

Confronted with her need for radical obedience, Esther sent a reply to Mordecai.

Go, gather together all the Jews who are in Susa [the capital city,] and fast for me. Do not eat or drink for three days, night or day. I and my maids will fast as you do. When this is done, I will go to the king, even though it is against the law. *And if I perish, I perish* (Esther 4:16, italics mine).

God honoured Esther for entrusting herself to him and the Jews were spared.

We are in a position similar to Esther's. There is no place for us as the Lord's daughters to argue with him. Phrases that begin with 'But' or 'You don't understand' are not ones used by a disciple of Jesus.

In the book of John, Jesus talks about the kernel of wheat (Jn 12:24). He says that it must fall to the ground and die in order to produce many seeds. Like Esther, we must let any faulty notions about ourselves fall to the ground and die. Through this action we may let God's truth bear the fruit of balanced femininity in our lives.

But what is God's design for true femininity? I find a full definition of femininity elusive. However, I do know that one crucial concept involves having a gentle and quiet spirit.

Where is my gentle and quiet spirit?

Many women feel condemned when they read 1 Peter 3:4: 'Instead, it should be that of your inner self, the unfading beauty of a gentle and quiet spirit, which is of great worth in God's sight.'

These women examine themselves and find that frustration, anger and anxiety dominate their lives. They may conclude that their gentle and quiet spirit lies deep within, buried under layers of old hurts. That is, of course, if their gentle and quiet spirit actually exists at all!

Over the past few years I have learned that a gentle and quiet spirit is a by-product of trust. Anxiety is the opposite of trust, and may manifest itself in aggressiveness and assertiveness. This usually occurs when a woman is relying on her own aptitude. In reality, trusting in oneself should produce anxiety! If we are trusting in self, we are operating in the flesh—depending on our limited resources—which includes all our old wounds and hurts. Consequently, old behaviour patterns re-emerge. In the wilds of Africa, a lion is never more dangerous than when it has been wounded! Likewise, when we are performing from a basis of unhealed hurt, our actions can prove dangerous to self and to others.

Numerous benefits are derived from trusting in God. I encourage you to begin with small steps and watch his faithfulness as he proves himself trustworthy. This will further encourage you to relinquish your own agenda and allow God to work deeply in your life. That inner beauty resulting from the inner peace you will experience, will be reflected in your character and in your outward demeanour.

From gender security toward real femininity

As a woman becomes secure in her gender, she automatically opens the door to femininity.

A good starting point in achieving gender security is to ask yourself pertinent questions. *What is my self-talk? Who do I say that I am?* Compare your thoughts of yourself with God's thoughts of you. Consciously reject all thoughts that do not measure up with the truth. This will take time. But change will take place if you combat your misbeliefs and replace them with God's truth. Let God affirm you. Make time each day just to sit in his presence. Again, this action will not come naturally, nor will it be easy to maintain at first. But perseverance will pay off.

Walking through the door to femininity can be awesome. It takes courage and determination to shed the old conception of oneself, and to embrace the emerging feminine self.

Recently, my friend Carol visited me for dinner. After the meal, we spent time perusing the photograph album she had brought. Struck by the obvious change in Carol's appearance over the past five years, I questioned her regarding the transformation.

'It wasn't as easy as grabbing a credit card and waltzing off to the shops,' she laughed. 'Actually, at times, it's been a pretty traumatic process.'

I nodded, reflected for a moment on my own journey, and then commented. 'I remember the sickening feeling when I realised that the next step in embracing my true femininity was to outwardly walk in the healing God had done in my life.'

'Yes,' agreed Carol. 'Part of me was content to stay in jeans and sweatshirts for the rest of my life. But I knew that my wardrobe choices could hold me back, almost locking me into an androgynous mindset.'

I walked across the room. 'Leanne Payne sums up what you are saying.' Pulling a book off the shelf, I shared with Carol a passage from *The Broken Image*.

The woman who can put on her feminine self (even though

she cannot herself sense it within) will find the exterior action stimulating the inner growth and maturation of her entire feminine being—emotional, intuitive, intellectual, and sensory.[15]

'Exactly,' agreed Carol. 'I found that as I began putting on dresses and experimenting with make-up, I created a framework in which God could work. He could bring my emotions in line with my outward appearance.'

'But this transformation didn't happen overnight, did it?' I asked.

'Oh, no!' Carol reflected for a moment. 'It all began three years ago. The leaders in my small group had arranged for a cosmetologist to come to an evening meeting. She arrived, armed with "war paint" and a selection of mirrors.'

'How did you feel as you were going through the whole make-up process?' I queried, recalling my first encounter with a bottle of foundation.

'Like a performing monkey. I detached emotionally. It was all too weird for me to fully comprehend in one sitting. When I finally looked in the mirror, I was horrified at the reflection. Not because the make-up looked bad—it didn't—but the person looking back at me was not me.

'I looked different—radically different—but I felt the same. Make-up didn't magically change my feelings; it merely highlighted the detachment I had always felt from everything feminine and soft.'

Carol paused, gathered herself, and continued. 'I allowed my eyes to focus steadily on this woman in the mirror. For the first time in my life I saw an outward reflection of my hidden self, the woman within. This feminine person had been suppressed for twenty-five years, and now I was looking at her. I questioned the face staring back at me. *Who are you? What do you want from me? What are you thinking?—What am I thinking?*'

A lump formed in my throat as Carol spoke.

'Immediately, I ran to the bathroom and wiped all the make-up off,' she continued. 'Later that night the four of us in the small group prayed for God to bring each one of us comfort and a sense of completion as we got in touch with this feminine part of ourselves.

'Over the subsequent weeks, I dabbled with make-up. I just began with a touch of mascara and blush. Nothing too drastic. With every step I began to feel more comfortable. 'Now I feel naked if I leave the house without make-up!' Carol chuckled.

'Dress for success'

I pointed to a photograph taken at a friend's wedding. 'But look at this picture. Look at the dress you're wearing. You *seem* to be really comfortable. Were you?'

'Yes, but that photograph was taken last year. I can show you some really awkward looking older photographs if you want.'

'No thanks,' I smiled. 'I've got plenty of my own.'

Carol looked quizzingly. 'I didn't know that you had difficulty wearing dresses.'

I looked at her incredulously. 'Who do you think I am—Elizabeth Taylor?' We laughed.

'Nothing in my healing process has come naturally to me,' I added. 'I still prefer to wear trousers rather than a dress, and that's okay. It's not essential that other people think I'm feminine. I feel my attitude towards—and acceptance of—myself, speaks for itself. I'm happy to be who I am.'

'Amen to that!' Carol agreed enthusiastically. 'But tell me more about your dress problems.'

'Well, it wasn't a big problem,' I continued. 'I just felt uncomfortable.'

'So what did you do?'

'I knew that I had to *feel* comfortable wearing a dress if I was to ever *look* comfortable in one. So I began by wearing a dress around the house. I would select certain days where I knew I would be alone, and I would spend it as a "woman".' I burst out laughing and added, 'Sort of like a female impersonator! Often I would be taken by surprise if I caught my reflection in the mirror, but, over a period of time, I grew used to seeing this new person. The next step was to present myself to the outside world.'

'Was that difficult for you?'

'It wasn't too hard in places like the shopping mall. No one knew me to care if I was wearing a dress or not. Interestingly, I found that shop assistants treated me differently.' I paused for a moment. 'Actually, maybe I treated them differently. Who knows?'

'What happened when you went to church?' Carol interrupted.

'That's where I encountered my first real difficulty. Putting on the dress and make-up was easy in comparison to receiving compliments regarding my actions. Compliments like, "Oh, you look pretty," were really hard to swallow. Friends were not stating the fact, like, "You are wearing a dress." They were commenting on the effect of my actions. Internally, my reaction was to disagree with their assessment. Words like pretty, attractive, and delightful were not adjectives I administered to myself.'

'But I hear you responding very graciously now when someone compliments you.'

'Yes, the breakthrough occurred when I was able to receive God's name for me, Woman. Since that point, I've made a conscious effort to embrace their compliments. There are still hurdles to cross in this whole area of gender identity and femininity. But the main barrier has been crossed. Realising that femininity wasn't a question of behaviour, but more a question of who God says I am, allowed me my quirks and idiosyncrasies without questioning my identity.'

A broad grin flashed across Carol's face. 'So I can continue to change my own car oil and still remain feminine?' she questioned.

'That's right!'

After Carol had left my apartment, I pulled another book off the shelf. Lois Mowday's *Daughters Without Dads* had helped clarify my thoughts on this subject. I turned to the page I had marked.

> So what is femininity? Femininity is an attitude rather than a list of characteristics. It is accepting me as me and not being defensive about who I am. Sometimes I am aggressive. Sometimes I am weak. Sometimes I confront, and sometimes I back down and cry. It depends on who we are as we stand before God. After we realise God has accepted us, then we can accept ourselves and others in a non-critical way.[16]

Lois Mowday allows for the individuality of each woman. Early on in my walk I had an irrational fear of becoming a Christian 'clone'. Faulty beliefs in God's ability to change each one of us in a different way fed my fear and subsequent resistance to change.

Biblical role models

The Bible, however, is filled with women who are marvellous, individualistic examples of real femininity.

Jesus' mother, Mary, is a wonderful example of trust, obedience and humility. She was willing to lay down her agenda for God to work through her. The depth of her faith is shown in her immediate response to the angelic message that she was to be divinely impregnated: ' "I am the Lord's servant," Mary answered. "May it be to me as you have said" ' (Lk 1:38).

Mary's response to God's command cannot have been easy. Undoubtedly, she had to withstand accusations of promiscuity and, because of her single status, her son's obvious illegitimacy. Exhibiting a God-centred life, Mary took strength in the belief that what the Lord had said to her would be accomplished. Despite all the sufferings Mary witnessed and experienced, she is found in the upper room praying with the rest of the disciples (Acts 1:14). This proves that she believed Jesus' claim to deity. She received him into her life. It is on that basis, and no other, that Mary obtained eternal life.

God's plan for our life brings ultimate blessing. Living in poverty and being an unmarried mother is not every little girl's dream for when she grows up. Our own dreams may be far-reaching and productive. But God may have other plans. Life may be hard for you at present. You may feel lost, possibly even abandoned at a critical time in your life. But humility, trust and obedience to God's plan all bring their own reward.

Miriam was a competent woman. She had a position of leadership in the exodus out of Egypt. This leadership was not only given to her because she was sister to Moses and Aaron, but because she was a prophetess in her own right.

When Miriam focused solely on God, she was elevated to the head of the assembly (Ex 15:20). Totally oblivious to self, she was able to dance and worship before the Lord. However, when Miriam fixed her eyes on her position— her standing in reference to Moses—envy and jealousy flourished. She became self-seeking and grumbled against Moses: 'One day Miriam and Aaron were criticising Moses because his wife was a Cushite woman, and they said, "Has the Lord spoken only through Moses? Hasn't he spoken through us, too?" ' (Num 12:1–2, TLB).

God always defends his chosen, and he struck Miriam with leprosy. It is interesting to note the contrast between walking in obedience and humility, and being self-seeking and rebellious. Moses' face was glorious and veiled to hide God's glory. The Hebrews were afraid to come near him. In contrast, Miriam's face was leprous and veiled to hide her shame. For seven days she was banished outside the camp and prohibited from being in fellowship with people.

When our focus is on God, we are content in our position. Discontent often results from the sin of comparison. Whether your position has many responsibilities or few, God will use your talents and abilities for his purpose when you desire to glorify him. He holds the key to your success. 'Keep looking up,' an old pastor once told me, 'unless you happen to be driving!'

A striking contrast in attitude can be found between Mary and Martha of Bethany. Mary sat at Jesus' feet, soaking up his love and teaching. She wanted to be in Jesus' company. Martha, however, was too concerned with activity. She obviously loved the Lord, but, unlike her sister, Martha placed service above devotion.

> But Martha was distracted by all the preparations that had to be made. She came to him and asked, 'Lord, don't you care that my sister has left me to do the work by myself? Tell her to help me!' 'Martha, Martha,' the Lord answered, 'you are worried and upset about many things, but only one thing is needed. Mary has chosen what is better, and it will not be taken away from her' (Lk 10:40–42).

Jesus desires a relationship with us, not service from us. If your abilities give you the sense of worth that you really should be receiving from your relationship with Jesus, then he will want to prune those abilities until you no longer hold onto them as idols. God has priorities. Service will flow out of the abundance of your relationship with him, not out of your need to feel worthy.

Present-day role models

We are not limited to historical feminine role models from the Bible. A woman coming out of homosexuality has much to learn through observing and imitating godly women in the church.

Joyce is a Christian, a wife, a mother, a deaconess and a bank manager. In her 'spare' time she organises hospital visitations and caters for church functions. Through self-control and discipline, Joyce has achieved much. But I have received a deeper understanding of femininity through observing Joyce's attitude toward others rather than focusing on her accomplishments. She observes those who are in need and seeks to minister to them. She is sensitive to those around her and takes delight in drawing out those less confident than herself. Joyce uses her talents for the benefit of others. She is not perfect, but her enthusiasm for the Lord is childlike and attracts people to her and to the Lord.

Emily prefers to remain behind the scenes. She is compassionate and sensitive. Beneath the gentle exterior is a woman who is determined to uphold God's standard in her home, with her family and in conversation with others. Still water certainly runs deep! Emily does not waver when confronted with ungodliness. When brought under the lordship of Christ, deep burning conviction manifests itself calmly and with clarity. I have learned, and am still learning, from Emily that there is no place for sarcasm, unbridled anger or hostility in a woman of God.

These two 'straight' women have taught me much about the practical aspects of femininity. However, it is important for us as ex-lesbians to know that many heterosexual women also struggle with the whole concept of femininity.

In leaving lesbianism behind, we need discernment to separate good role models, like Joyce and Emily, from those women who also need help in the area of broken femininity. But often we are unable to distinguish the characteristics we see in other women which are good, and therefore worthy of imitation, and the characteristics which are bad, and therefore need to be rejected. Out of our own brokenness, it is easy to fall prey to the thought: *They are married and have children. Surely they must be totally whole and healthy.* Nothing could be further from the truth!

Insecurity and dependence, anger and independence, are not the champions of the homosexual only. These problems also run rampant in the heterosexual community.

Many women who struggle with insecurity and dependence are often submissive to the point of self-abasement. They tend to be people-pleasers in order to obtain a measure of self-worth. Often the church mistakenly attributes these flaws as displays of charity, humility and a gentle spirit.

Other women struggle with anger and independence. They may appear somewhat aloof, maybe even intimidating. They tend to compete with rather than complement men. Often behind this competent exterior is someone who lacks confidence that she will be accepted as a woman. Or she may believe, consciously or subconsciously, that masculine roles and activities are more important and provide a greater security than feminine roles. Often, at the root of her problems is unexpressed, unresolved anger, frequently based on childhood wounding.

Do these women sound somewhat like yourself?

A startling revelation came when I discovered that heterosexual women did not float through life on gossamer wings. Although they did not share my particular gender confusion, many operated out of a greater sense of feminine brokenness than I did. This understanding enabled me to bring my homosexual struggles into perspective. I could discern what was inherently a lesbian problem, what was inherently a feminine problem, and what was intrinsically a 'people' problem.

Am I alone in my walk?

Satan would have you believe that you are to walk your own path for the rest of your life. Nothing could be further from the truth.

I used to dream that I was a traveller. Picturing myself standing on the platform of a railway station, I noted that my bags were packed and my hand clutched a ticket that read, 'Female'. A train pulled in—destination: femininity. The conductress sounded the 'all aboard'.

I wanted desperately to join the women on this train, but as I tried to step forward, my feet seemed cemented into place. The last call came, I could not budge, and the train pulled away from the station without me.

Soon, another train glided into the platform. 'All the rest aboard,' the conductress shouted. No hesitation this time. My feet bounded up the steps. I expected to find myself alone in the coach, but surprise, surprise! I found a whole group of women like me. Some were married, some were widowed or divorced, and others were single. There were lesbians on the train, and there were straight women. Each of us had one thing in common: we were bound for the land of 'The Faulty Feminine'.

I no longer have that dream.

For further study

1. *Inside Out* by Larry Crabb (NavPress: USA [and UK], 1988).
2. *The Broken Image: Restoring Personal Wholeness Through Healing Prayer* by Leanne Payne (Crossway Books: 1981) (UK edition: Kingsway Publications, 1988).
3. *Daughters Without Dads* by Lois Mowday (Oliver-Nelson: USA, 1990).

Moving Towards
the Land of Promise

CHAPTER TWELVE

SPIRITUAL WARFARE

Choosing to leave the lesbian life brings us into direct conflict with the satanic realm. While we were enmeshed in dependency or sexual sin, we were of little problem to Satan, because sin paralyses our effectiveness as a Christian. We may have vocalised allegiance to God, but our actions proved to the contrary. Only when we understand and implement spiritual warfare can our walk into wholeness be successful.

What are we fighting?

The Bible clearly states that we are not in combat against flesh and blood. Our enemy is not found in the ranks of gay activist groups or the Metropolitan Community Church, although both may be used as instruments of Satan. Ephesians 6:12 states that we are: 'against the rulers, against the authorities, against the powers of this dark world and against the spiritual forces of evil in the heavenly realms.'

We are the victims of invisible forces, but we can be the victors through Christ. For the woman seeking change, attack comes from three sides: Satan, the world and the flesh.

Satan

The Bible refers to Satan as a liar and a murderer. He is described as the destroyer (Jn 10:10), someone who lays waste whatever stands in his way. He tries to distort, twist, and counterfeit all of God's creation. He emphasises illusion through fantasy. Fantasy, whether limited to one's mind or actually acted upon, ultimately creates disappointment because real life can never match our fantasies. Moreover, Satan immediately introduces guilt and condemnation. The book of Revelation classifies him as the deceiver of the whole world (Rev 12:9). Other passages tell us that he is 'the evil one' (Mt 13:38), the 'god of this age' (2 Cor 4:4), the 'tempter' (1 Thess 3:5) and the 'accuser of our brothers' (Rev 12:10).

These names do not lack substance. They should educate us in the way Satan works, so that we will not be 'unaware of his schemes' (2 Cor 2:11).

He can attack us as a roaring lion, bounding into full view with fangs bared. Or he can allure us, appearing as an angel of light who offers us false hope and satisfaction, but then leaves us empty and discontent.

The world

In our world today, walking away from the sin of homosexuality is not easy. Holy and righteous living is not encouraged; quite the contrary. While living in the San Francisco area of California, I was bombarded with pro-gay material from every angle. Not only was homosexuality openly expressed in several city districts, it was the subject of positive discrimination in all aspects of the media. In a three-day time frame, I watched a television programme funded by the gay and lesbian population of San Francisco, encountered a large photograph of two gay men illustrating the cover story of the largest newspaper in Northern California, and was confronted with a photograph of a gay couple in the marriage section of another newspaper. They were standing outside a Metropolitan Community Church having exchanged vows. The couple, we are told, honeymooned in France.

Parents who are against the current increase of pro-gay action within public schools, are labelled as homophobic, and Christian ministries helping those men and women who *want* release from homosexuality, are accused of being 'brainwashing guilt-mongers'.

On a personal note, I have been accused in print and on television of being misguided and deluded. Opponents accuse me of merely suppressing my 'natural' desires. 'Change is not possible!' they claim loudly.

Opposition to righteous living is strong, but we can be assured of success when we read Acts 5:38–39: 'For if their purpose or activity is of human origin, it will fail. But if it is from God, you will not be able to stop these [women]; you will only find yourselves fighting against God.'

Change, when motivated and empowered by God, is possible. God has called us out of darkness and into his light. But we cannot look to the world to endorse our commitment to God, nor to applaud our journey out of lesbianism.

The flesh

Perhaps the flesh is the most subtle of our three enemies. This urge towards self-centredness is manifested through wilful defiance and rebellion. The term backsliding— turning away from God—succinctly describes a situation we can find ourselves in without really trying! The move away from God can happen so subtly, so silently, that we suddenly find ourselves deep in dependency or rampant lust, confused as to how we ever got there.

The Bible lists a number of warning signs which indicate a movement away from God:

> Impure thoughts, eagerness for lustful pleasure, idolatry, spiritism (that is, encouraging the activity of demons), hatred and fighting, jealousy and anger, constant effort to get the best for yourself, complaints and criticisms, the feeling that everyone else is wrong except those in your own little group—and there will be wrong doctrine, envy, murder, drunkenness, wild parties, and all that sort of thing (Gal 5:19–21, TLB).

Backsliding occurs because we are bent on following our desires, rather than God's guidelines. The end result is clear.

> But each one is tempted when, by his own evil desire, he is dragged away and enticed. Then, after desire has conceived, it gives birth to sin; and sin, when it is full-grown, gives birth to death (Jas 1:14–15).

Problems of the flesh can never be solved by fleshly means. Our methods merely rearrange the problem, rather than dismantle it. For instance, a woman may overcome her compulsive masturbation, but then find herself caught up in a cycle of compulsive overeating. The basic problem of seeking comfort through fleshly means has not disappeared; it has merely taken on a new face. True change occurs from the inside out, as we allow Jesus to mould and reshape us.

The spirit, the soul and the body

God and Satan work through the same channels: the spirit, the soul and the body. Although each channel is separate in its own function, each is linked to the others.

When Christ is the centre of your life, your spirit, soul and body work in unison to the glory of God. In your spirit, there is security knowing Christ has granted you salvation. You recognise your body as a temple of the Holy Spirit. And your soul—thoughts, emotions and decision-making—are prompted by God.

Conversely, when self runs your life, Satan will attack you spiritually by questioning your salvation, security and commitment to God. He offers illegitimate solutions to gratify physical desires and needs (sex before marriage, for example), which wreaks havoc on your mind, emotions and will. Consequently, pride, fear and self-seeking will consume you.

Although God and Satan use the same channels, they have different intentions. God knits the spirit, soul and body in harmony and balance. Satan creates discord between the three areas. God offers faith, which is based in hope and love. Satan offers fear, which only brings discouragement and defeat.

Understanding Ephesians 6:13–17

It had been several months since Tessa first came to me for help. Although her enthusiasm to receive healing from lesbianism was unabated, her Christian walk lacked stability. Some days Tessa was bubbly and full of joy, other days she was low and full of doubt.

'Tessa,' I asked, during a private counselling session, 'have you ever received any teaching on Ephesians 6:13–17?'

I handed her a sheet of paper with the relevant Scripture and sat quietly while she read it.

Therefore, put on the full armour of God, so that when the day of evil comes, you may be able to stand your ground, and after you have done everything, to stand. Stand firm then, with the belt of truth buckled around your waist, the breastplate of righteousness in place, and with your feet fitted with the readiness that comes from the gospel of peace. In addition to this, take up the shield of faith, with which you can extinguish all the flaming arrows of the evil one. Take the helmet of salvation and the sword of the Spirit, which is the word of God (Eph 6:13–17).

Tessa looked up, scrunched up her nose and shook her head. 'Nah,' she drawled. 'I've read it a couple of times, but I can't remember hearing a sermon about it.'

'Okay,' I replied. 'Then today's session is on spiritual warfare. An understanding of the resources you have available to you and how to use them will help stabilise your walk with the Lord.'

'Great!' Tessa exclaimed. 'My Christian walk feels as though I'm traversing the Rocky Mountain Range—all peaks and valleys! I'd appreciate something a little more level.'

I took out my notes on spiritual warfare, prayed for clarity and began my explanation. 'The first thing to understand is that Jesus is our armour. He is our defence. We no longer have to find ways of defending ourselves, we have to implement all that He has provided.

'There are three pieces of armour which were given at our conversion. According to the verse you just read in Ephesians, we have put on the belt of truth, put on the breastplate of righteousness, and put on the shoes of readiness that comes from peace.'

'What does that mean?' asked Tessa.

I motioned for Tessa to sit next to me so that she could follow my notes.

The Belt of Truth. We are to align ourselves with the

word of God. The Bible tells us that Jesus is the same yesterday, today and tomorrow. Knowing that God loves us and is on our side means that we can trust him and what is written in the Bible. We need this strong base of support to withstand the schemes of Satan.

The Breastplate of Righteousness. We do not stand on our own merits. We never did. The breastplate enables us to stand because of the righteousness of Jesus. He is our grounding before God. The breastplate protects us from those emotions which challenge our standing before God—self-condemnation or pride.

The Shoes of Peace. Peace is a natural result of standing on the merits of Christ. Our trust is in him and he will not fail us. Circumstances may not have changed, and temptation may not have ceased, but this peace passes all understanding. Peace in our heart enables us to stand.

Tessa thought for a moment. 'This sounds great, Jeanette. But how can I apply these verses when I am being attacked by Satan?'

'Let's say you are undergoing great temptation to return to the lesbian life. Perhaps you crave the mental, emotional and physical comfort of another woman. You know that it would be wrong to act upon these desires and are valiantly seeking God's answer to this dilemma.'

Tessa nodded.

'At the height of this struggle, you sense Satan tempting you. He's whispering things like: "You deserve some comfort, you've had a rough day. Who says it's wrong? It feels right, doesn't it?"

'Then, once you've succumbed to the temptation, Satan immediately becomes the accuser: "Call yourself a Christian when you still act like this? You haven't changed! You're just kidding yourself!" '

Tessa cringed. 'Stop it, Jeanette. I know exactly what you're talking about.'

Many of us have had the same experience. The point I'm trying to make is that we can let Jesus defend us with the armour we have been given. We are wearing the belt of truth. Tessa, what does the word say that would help you at this point?'

Scratching her head, Tessa thought for a while. Finally she answered. 'It tells us that there is no temptation that is not common to all of us [1 Cor 10:13]. So it's a comfort to know that we are not alone in this struggle. The word also tells us that we can call on the name of the Lord, and he *will* hear us [Ps 86:7]. And regarding Satan's accusation that we haven't changed, 2 Corinthians 5:17 says: "Therefore, if anyone is in Christ, he is a new creation; the old has gone, the new has come!"'

'Wow, I was actually able to quote a relevant verse from memory,' laughed Tessa.

'That's great, Tess,' I said, encouraged by her ability to utilise Scripture verses for her own immediate benefit. 'Remember, Jesus didn't bother discussing anything with Satan in Luke 4. He simply countered Satan's accusations with Scripture.

'We have other pieces of armour to help us. The breastplate of righteousness prevents us from succumbing emotionally to the accusations of Satan [Rom 8:1]. You know, he's right when he says that we don't deserve to be called a Christian.'

Tessa looked stunned.

'If it was based solely on *our* merit, we wouldn't be able to call ourselves Christians. But fortunately we don't have to rely on that. Jesus is our righteousness. We only have to rely on him.'

Tessa visibly relaxed, and I continued.

'Knowing that we have the word and Jesus actively on our side should give us the peace I spoke about earlier. We can choose to ignore Satan's accusations because we remember our true position in Christ. We are not fighting alone, and we are not on the losing side. We are victorious.'

I paused a moment, then continued. 'There are three other pieces of armour that we are to utilise. What are they?'

Tessa re-read the Scripture. 'We are to take the shield of faith, take the helmet of salvation and take the sword of the Spirit. They are all actions I have to do.'

'Right,' I agreed. 'These three new pieces are what I must claim and use. The Bible refers to Satan's accusations as being "fiery darts". Lewd thoughts, flashbacks, fears and anxieties all come under that title. The enemy's darts almost appear to be coming from within us and they attack our position as a Christian. The darts question the validity of Christ as the truth, the true position of Christ as my righteousness, and, consequently, they destroy our peace.'

'Well, I've certainly been stabbed by his darts quite a bit recently,' Tessa remarked.

'In what ways?' I probed.

'Mainly, through memories. Late one night last week, I was in bed reading the newspaper when I suddenly remembered Sharon, an ex-lover from years ago. Why? She would always read the paper in bed before going to sleep, no matter how late the hour. It wouldn't have been so bad if the memory stopped there, but it didn't. Before I knew it, I was inundated with all kinds of memories involving Sharon. It was a rough night. All because of one lousy newspaper! Is there anything I can do about it?'

'You've posed another question, Tess,' I replied. 'Where does temptation stop and the woman's responsibility begin?'

Tessa looked puzzled.

'The initial memory regarding Sharon was a fiery dart, as you didn't intentionally decide to think about her. But you didn't immediately come against the memory either. It sounds like your passivity in standing against your thought life encouraged further memories. Hence your difficult night.'

Tessa shot me an angry glance. 'It's my fault?' She slumped back in the armchair, folded her arms and sulked. 'I give up. This is too difficult!'

Knowing that Tessa's moods were brief, I continued. 'By using the shield of faith you can help prevent that from happening again.' I showed Tessa my notes.

The Shield of Faith. Faith cannot exist in a vacuum, it must act on belief. Faith can be split into three segments:

1. Decision
2. Resolution
3. Action

'Let's use the example regarding your thought life,' I proceeded. 'A memory of Sharon occurs. What do you do with it? Do you allow yourself self-centred thoughts? *I'll never get my needs met. I feel lonely. I deserve a little indulgence.* Or do you line your thoughts up with God?'

1. Decision—Jesus will meet my every need.
2. Resolution—I will not entertain my past memories.
3. Action—I will put down the newspaper and play a praise tape.

Tessa looked up. 'But even that seems too difficult right now.'

'It takes time to form new habits, Tess,' I said gently. 'Just saying "no" isn't enough. We need to replace old patterns with new ones. Singing a praise song, praying out loud or reading Scripture renders old thoughts ultimately ineffective. The Bible also says that if we resist Satan he *will* flee from us [Jas 4:7].'

By now, Tessa was leaning forward in her seat. She was beginning to understand that she had options when confronted with temptations, accusations or old memories. I pointed back at my notes, and we continued reading.

The Helmet of Salvation protects our mind. It keeps our thinking ordered and preserves us from mental confusion and darkness. Although there are skirmishes that we sometimes lose, the helmet reminds us of the overall picture. Hebrews 2:8–9 states: 'Yet at present we do not see everything subject to him. But we see Jesus.'

Tessa sat bolt upright. 'I've just thought of another Scripture,' she exclaimed.

We demolish arguments and every pretension that sets itself up against the knowledge of God, and we take captive every thought to make it obedient to Christ (2 Cor 10:5).

'That would keep our thinking ordered, wouldn't it?' Tessa asked eagerly.

'Yes,' I agreed. 'And our focus is to be kept on the author and perfecter of our faith. If our focus is on people and circumstances, we will take off our helmet of salvation.'

'Then we're open to Satan's fiery darts,' interjected Tessa. 'Wow, this is great! So often I find myself getting bogged down with various areas of my healing. I know I forget to look up and focus on Jesus. Until now, I didn't realise the consequence of that action. I ought to have signs posted to remind me. You know, like they have on building sites: "Danger—Hard Hat Area"!'

I laughed. It was hard not to like Tessa.

'Now for the sword,' I said, pointing to the next section of my notes.

The Sword of the Spirit. The sword of the Spirit is
the word of God. Hebrews 4:12 states: 'For the word of
God is living and active. Sharper than any double-edged
sword, it penetrates even to dividing soul and spirit,
joints and marrow.'

'Let's look at an example,' I proceeded. 'I'm feeling
vulnerable. I feel oppressed by Satan, and overwhelmed
by the bombardment of his fiery darts. I'm beginning to
believe his lies that I'm lonely and unloved. I am helpless
and hopeless. Now, what Scripture would best help me in
this situation?'

Tessa's brow furrowed. 'This is hard, Jeanette. You
keep putting me on the spot,' she moaned.

'Think.'

After a few seconds, her eyes twinkled. 'I know. "He
who is in me is greater than he who is in the world." '

'What does that mean to you?' I asked, knowing that
quoting Scripture does not always solve a problem unless
it is applied in a practical way.

'It means that I don't have to lie down and die,' said
Tessa. 'I have the power through the Holy Spirit to over-
come this depression. Oh! I've just thought of another
Scripture that would help me. Isaiah 61 says that I will be
given "a garment of praise instead of a spirit of despair".
That would help me, wouldn't it?'

'Yes, provided that you implement it. Again, you could
put on a praise tape and join in the singing. Or you could
audibly thank God for all the blessings he has given you
thus far. Well done, Tessa.'

Grinning smugly, Tessa sat back in the armchair as I
proceeded. 'The sword of the Spirit is useful for defense or
offense. We can parry or thrust, depending on the need.
But, if we don't read the Bible and act upon what we read,
we are exposing ourselves to defeat and despair. We are in

a battle without the necessary power. We are as good as dead.'

A quizzical expression flitted over Tessa's face. 'Jeanette, this passage in Ephesians keeps telling me to stand. Why?'

'If you read carefully, it tells us that we are only able to stand *after* we are wearing the armour. It means that we must refuse to move from the ground of faith we have taken. Sometimes, warfare is so intense that all we can do is stand. Attacks come from circumstances, fearful situations, indifference on our part and the world. We are not to take new ground, but to defend that which is already ours. We have been given a new life in Christ, the fullness and wholeness promised in the word. Christ has already accomplished everything. Our job is to stand secure in that victory.'

Tessa left the office that day feeling less like a victim and more like an overcomer. She had tools which she could implement when attacked by Satan, the world and her own flesh. More importantly, Tessa left with the understanding that she was not a pawn in some heavenly battle, but a soldier fighting a war that has already been won.

Beware of compromise

Spiritual battles are fought on many fronts. One of these fronts is compromise. Compromising the word of God is always a backward step in our Christian walk. Moses had to face this problem in Egypt. God had clearly told him to take all of the Hebrew people into the desert so that they could offer sacrifices up to God. This action did not please Pharaoh, and he offered an alternative to God's command. 'Then Pharaoh summoned Moses and Aaron and said, "Go, sacrifice to your God here in the Land" ' (Ex 8:25).

What do we hear today? The call to compromise reaches our ears: 'Certainly, you can be a Christian. But you don't have to stop being a lesbian just because you want to worship God. Do both. Don't be so fanatical in your Christianity. After all, you're only doing what comes naturally, aren't you?'

But God calls us to separate ourselves. Light and darkness cannot mingle. We will either influence the world, or be influenced by the world.

When Moses refused to accept the first compromise, Pharaoh submitted a new proposal. 'Pharaoh said, "I will let you go to offer sacrifices to the LORD your God in the desert, but you must not go very far" ' (Ex 8:28).

Similarly, some lesbians in a pang of conviction will walk away from their sin, but are loathe to wander too far away. They stay in touch with gay friends, hold onto mementos, or continue to read gay books and magazines. These women stay close enough to return to their lesbian life once the fright of conviction is over. They vacillate between conviction and corruption, trying to maintain a precarious balance between the two. The nation of Israel fell into the same trap.

When Moses refused the second offer in his determination to obey God's command in full, Pharaoh devised another sneaky alternative. 'Pharaoh said, "The LORD be with you—if I let you go, along with your women and children! Clearly you are bent on evil. No! Have only the men go" ' (Ex 10:10–11).

We are easily caught in a similar type of compromise. 'No one is stopping you from going to church on Sunday!' say our gay friends. But disaster comes when we worship God on Sunday and feed our lives with the influences of our past life during the rest of the week. If we are to break free from the bondage of lesbianism, we must follow God with our whole heart, mind and strength. We must be women who are wholly committed to God.

One must give Pharaoh credit for perseverance! 'Then Pharaoh summoned Moses and said, "Go, worship the

LORD. Even your women and children may go with you; only leave your flocks and herds behind" ' (Ex 10:24).

Similarly, women struggling with lesbianism tend to bargain with God. 'OK, I'll give up having sex, but don't ask me to leave my (mutually dependent) friend.' We tend to choose which sin we will or will not leave behind.

There is no place for compromise. God will not share your heart with the world and your flesh. Only a complete break with your past, leaving Egypt fully behind, will bring healing in your life.

You cannot go it alone!

Deciding to leave our past sinful life is no easy task, and to enter into something new is often very frightening. We need help. This comes in a variety of forms: through basic fellowship at church, specialised support groups, tapes and newsletters from pertinent ministries, Christian books on homosexuality and specific conferences, such as the annual Exodus conferences in North America, Europe and the South Pacific. As I stated earlier in chapter 10, we need small groups to hold us accountable and give us support.

We can look back to the exodus story to help illustrate the need for support. Not long after the Hebrews left Egypt, the Amalekites subjected them to an unprovoked attack.

> So Joshua fought the Amalekites as Moses had ordered, and Moses, Aaron and Hur went to the top of the hill. As long as Moses held up his hands, the Israelites were winning, but whenever he lowered his hands, the Amalekites were winning. When Moses hands grew tired, they took a stone and put it under him, and he sat on it. Aaron and Hur held his hands up—one on one side, one on the other—so that his hands remained steady until sunset. So Joshua overcame the Amalekite army with the sword (Ex 17:10–13).

We must always seek the Lord with regard to the method that we use to combat the enemy. When the Egyptians pursued the Hebrews, God called his people to stand and watch what he would do. In that instance, he parted the Red Sea—no small gesture! Now, some months later, the Amalekites are the enemies. This time, God calls the Hebrews to fight.

The meaning for Joshua is 'The Lord is Salvation'. Joshua was promoted to commander-in-chief of the army to lead the Hebrews into battle. Moses, on the other hand, climbed a hill to watch the war. His purpose was to intercede for the warriors.

Jesus assumes both of these roles in our own battles. He leads us against our enemies while also interceding for us, seated at God's right hand.

Moses also held up his hands as a reminder of past victories (the ten plagues; the parting of the Red Sea; bringing drinking water to the people). The Hebrew warriors were able to look up in the midst of the battle, see Moses' arms lifted high and remember past triumphs accomplished by God's power. In the midst of our trials, it is good to look up and remind ourselves of all the past struggles God has brought us through.

As Moses raised his arms, we should also lift our arms to God. I say this for two reasons: first, as a form of worship to give him our praise; and second, to receive all that he has to shower upon us. But Moses' arms failed, reminding us that all warfare is exhausting. We need to be strong in faith and prayer. But we also need to ask for support from others and be gracious enough to receive all that is offered.

Aaron and Hur could only offer a stone for Moses to sit on for the day. A more comfortable chair would have been preferable, but a stone was sufficient. Similarly, you may desire a support group specifically for ex-gays, but your church can only offer you a general Bible study. Humble yourself and gratefully accept whatever is available. God does not need programmes and specific teachings to work in your life. I had been away from the lesbian life for nearly three years before I knew that ex-gay ministries existed. But I experienced significant growth in those three years.

Aaron and Hur held up Moses' arms for the duration of the day. That was hard work. We also need praying warriors around us in our struggle. It is important, too, that we are an 'Aaron' for someone else. Offer yourself as a prayer warrior. It is not enough to receive. We need also to submit our spiritual services to others.

Moses makes a memorial

After the victory over the Amalekites, Moses built an altar. He called it *Jehovah Nissi* — 'The Lord is My Banner'. Moses recognised the Hebrews' complete dependence on God throughout the whole battle.

We are no different than Moses. Whatever happens in our lives, whatever victories are won, and whatever healing takes place, the glory must go to God. His name belongs on our victory banner. 'For it is by grace you have been saved, through faith—and this not from yourselves, it is the gift of God—not by works, so that no man can boast' (Eph 2:8–9).

Memorials are powerful reminders. Various kinds of memorials abound in the Bible, but they fall into three basic categories:

1. *Something you do*. In the Old Testament times, a servant who loved his master could have his ear pierced with an awl against the doorpost of his master's home. He then became a voluntary slave for life. The pierced ear served as a permanent reminder of the servant's love for his master (see Ex 21:2–6). Another biblical example is

the Lord's Supper (communion), a visible reminder of God's work on our behalf.

2. *Something you say*. God often changed a person's name after a significant event in their life. For instance, He changed Abram to Abraham—'exalted father' to 'father of a great number'.

3. *Something you make*. Altars to worship the Lord were the most common example of this type of memorial. The Israelites built an altar after they crossed the Jordan River to enter the land that God had promised them.

Some memorials need to be destroyed. The Bible reiterates the need to pull down the Ashteroth poles, the altars to idols and the high places that are set up in direct opposition to God. We experience new freedom when we destroy old memorials, such as movies, books and clothes which keep us locked in a sinful, idolatrous mindset. Once the old mementos (idols) are gone, they can be replaced with new memorials erected to the glory of God.

Memorials can be a great encouragement, a reminder that there is hope for now and for the future based on what God has done in the past. This book is my memorial. Irrespective of whatever happens with me in the future, I have a memorial of God's work in my life. Of course, one does not have to go to the extreme of writing a book in order to create a memorial. For instance, keeping a journal is an ongoing memorial to God. Recording all that he has done in your life is a tribute to his faithfulness, goodness and mercy.

I have a friend who highly recommends creative memorials. 'When I least expect it and most need it,' he told me, 'God uses one of my memorials to spark a renewed vision of hope when I'm feeling weary, or bring a smile following a time of intense sadness, or even a tear in the midst of a joyful period.'

He shared with me some practical ideas for memorials.

- Create a photo album, scrapbook or photo collage of significant people and events the Lord has brought into your life.
- Pick out a favourite Scripture verse that encourages you in the 'down times' and design a banner with this verse to hang on your wall.
- Write a poem or song about a specific time that God provided for your need.
- Keep a diary of specific prayers God has answered. Include the date you started praying, the request, when you noted his answer, and how he answered.
- Did God provide for a financial need in a dramatic (or even non-dramatic) way? Photocopy the cheque, save the coins you got as change, or photograph what God gave you.
- Don't keep an event to yourself. If God involved your friends in any way to accomplish his will, discuss with them various ways you can memorialise the events and thus remember them.
- Mark your calendar for a once-a-month Memorial Day celebration. All month long, write down on index cards the important things God has done for you or has been teaching you. Include the date and a brief description. On your celebration day, pull out all the cards from that month and read them. Better yet, include friends in your celebration and have them also read aloud from their index cards.

I am sure you can come up with creative ideas of your own. Whatever you do, use your memorials to praise God and give him the glory for all he has done in your life.

Praise can be a powerful antidote to trials and tribulations that come your way in the spiritual battle.

Overcoming your spiritual enemies

In Revelation 12:11 we read: 'They overcame him by the blood of the Lamb and by the word of their testimony; they did not love their lives so much as to shrink from death.'

We can become an overcomer only through Christs' death—the blood of the Lamb. The word of our testimony, a memorial to his work, is built on this foundation. Being an overcomer means offering a sacrificial memorial to God by yielding our hopes and desires to him.

Spiritual warfare is an everyday reality. Satan tries to render us ineffective, but we can don the armour of God and stand our ground. Coming out of lesbianism *is* possible as we fight the battle in God's strength.

For further study

1. *This Present Darkness* by Frank Peretti (Crossway Books: USA, 1986) (UK edition: Monarch Publications, 1989).
2. *Piercing the Darkness* by Frank Peretti (Crossway Books: USA, 1990) (UK edition: Monarch Publications, 1990).
3. *The Adversary* by Mark Bubeck (Moody Press: USA).
4. *Overcoming the Adversary* by Mark Bubeck (Moody Press: USA).
5. *Handbook to Happiness* by Charles Solomon (Tyndale House: USA).
6. *The Beautiful Side of Evil* by Johanna Michelson (Harvest House: USA).
7. *The Theatre of Your Mind* by Denny Gunderson (LD#73—Last Days Ministries, PO Box, Lindale, TX 75771-0040, USA).

8. *The Bondage Brakers* by Neil Anderson (Harvest House: USA, 1990).
9. *Victory Over Darkness* by Neil Anderson (Regal Books: USA, 1990).

Resources if you have been in the occult or Eastern religions

Spiritual Counterfeits Project
PO Box 4308
Berkeley, CA 94704
USA
office phone: (415) 540-0300

Christian Research Institute, International
(founded by the late Dr Walter Martin)
PO Box 500
San Juan Capistrano, CA 92693-0500
USA
office phone: (714) 855-9926

also

Deo Gloria Trust
Selsdon House
212–220 Addington Road
South Croydon
Surrey CR2 8LD, UK
Tel: 081 651 6428

CHAPTER THIRTEEN

CLEFT OF THE ROCK: GLIMPSES OF GOD'S GOODNESS

Even though Moses was intimate with God, he desired more of his presence and asked God to show him his glory. God knew that Moses would be unable to see the fullness of his glory—the effect would be too much for anyone. But God did make provision for his friend.

> Then the LORD said, 'There is a place near me where you may stand on a rock. When my glory passes by, I will put you in a cleft in the rock and cover you with my hand until I have passed by. Then I will remove my hand and you will see my back; but my face must not be seen' (Ex 33:21–23).

We can learn from Moses' example. No matter how devoted we are, we can never get too close to God. But our position is not the same as Moses. Today, we are able to stand on the rock, Jesus, and hide in him. Colossians 3:3 states: 'For you have died, and your life is hid with Christ in God' (RSV).

Through salvation we, too, are able to rest in the cleft of the rock. By remaining in Jesus we are protected from the punishment due us through our sinful disposition. As we yield our lives to him, we see more of his glory—God's goodness towards us.

This chapter comprises testimonies from four of my friends who have also left the lesbian life and are pressing on towards wholeness in Christ. They are witnesses of God's goodness toward those who are obedient to his calling. I have asked the women to focus not on their past sin, but on the work God has done and is doing in their lives right now. I pray that you will be encouraged by their stories.

Deborah's story

Over the two short years that I've been actively in the healing process, God has totally blown me away by his faithfulness. He has given back exceedingly above and beyond my wildest unspoken dreams.

I was the last child and only daughter in a large family. Within five years of my birth, three of my siblings died.

My parents were very emotionally broken people who did the best they could. However, that doesn't change the reality that my father was very passive, a non-abusive alcoholic. My mother avoided the pain in her own life by being irresponsibly generous. Also, she was very talkative, but only on surface issues. Mum just couldn't share deeply—her denial of emotions was too great. Consequently, we were a household of emotionally autistic people.

Ours was a typical alcoholic family. Dad abdicated his responsibilities, so Mum assumed his role. But there were no rules, no limits, no boundaries placed upon me by either parent. 'Just let us know where you are and what you want to do,' was all I heard.

My detachment from my family began essentially at birth, when I was separated from Mum due to jaundice, a reaction to a blood Rh-factor problem. My childhood was fairly traumatic. When I was thirteen months old, I was scalded with coffee. Second- and third-degree burns covered over sixty per cent of my body. Though I have no memory of it, that same year I witnessed my thirteen-year-old brother accidentally shoot and kill my eleven-year-old brother.

Sexual abuse and incest came up numerous times when I was young. One brother abused me a couple of times when I was only four and five years old. Later on, a family friend molested me sexually, as did this same brother plus a buddy of his. A middle-aged stranger molested me while swimming in a lake when I was ten. Although my family was right on the shore within eyesight, I didn't know that I could call them for help.

At age seven, I simultaneously developed stress-related ulcers, pneumonia, and other medical problems which meant more hospital time. From then through age thirteen, I was hospitalised at least once a year for pneumonia. Sadly, the hospital was the only secure environment I can remember while growing up.

All these molestations, coupled with the shame of growing up with a leering, lecherous uncle who always made me feel naked in his presence, left me with a rather warped perception of myself, men, women and sex. I believe my basic coping method was to view everyone as genderless, assume an arrogantly independent attitude, and subconsciously avoid men as much as possible.

Growing up, I didn't feel attracted to either sex. I dated a couple of guys, but didn't allow my emotions to be involved. The relationships were platonic. Thus, I always felt I had control over the situation.

When I was eighteen, I rented a room in the house of one of my professors. Another guy living there had just broken up with his girlfriend. He began to initiate a relationship with me, but I was keenly aware that he just wanted an 'interim fix' while his girlfriend got over her anger.

This guy was not subtle in his invitations. He straight out asked me if I'd like to 'make love'. I kept declining, but finally let him kiss me. Unexpectedly, I felt myself powerfully responding to him. But then he commented, 'I gotcha,' and everything turned to icy stone inside of me. I would not yield control any further. This man would not win. I would not be used and then discarded! I slammed the door on my emotional and physical response with finality.

Less than a year later, my first emotional dependency began with a girlfriend. It dragged on for five years, in spite of emotional and physical abuse between us. My eight years' experience in homosexuality involved gross emotional dependency which led to sexual relationships with a string of lesbian lovers.

Now I realise there were two key factors in my struggles with emotional dependency.

- Having no sense of personal boundaries, which stemmed from the alcoholic family setting and the sexual abuse.
- Longing to be protected.

On the issue of protection, from the time I was very young I figured I'd have to look after myself. I simply didn't know of any other option. In fact, not until I was twenty-eight years old and in my first year at an ex-gay live-in program in California, did I ever even hear of the concept of being protected. One room-mate spoke of feeling unprotected and I couldn't understand what she was talking about. I had no point of reference—I never knew such a thing existed to be able to miss it. Ironically, the only family member who said he'd look after me and defend me was the brother who molested me.

When Dad said that he 'would never hurt me', I interpreted that to mean he would not force me into an incestuous relationship. He kept his promise. Dad never 'hurt me' in that way. But I never remember being hugged or affirmed by him. He never told me, 'I love you.' In 1979 Dad had a stroke and he couldn't communicate much after that. He died in 1985. We didn't know each other. In fact, until recently it seemed like he had never lived or had any impact on my life. In 1989 I experienced a brief amount of grieving for his death, but God has not yet begun to deal directly with my father/daughter issues.

I became a Christian in the autumn of 1983, but my 'crash and burn cycle' of emotional dependency continued to repeat itself until 1988. By then I realised this cycle wouldn't be broken without a major catalyst. I still had not accepted the fact that homosexuality was an issue in my life. I merely considered myself an opportunist, and if I happened to 'fall in love' with a woman, c'est la vie.

This sin cycle itself didn't bother me, but rather the fact that it kept blocking my walk with God. I really wanted to know him, but didn't know there was anything I could do about my sinful patterns. Then God, in his perfect timing and incredible love, set up a 'divine appointment'. The time was ripe for me to begin facing my lesbianism.

On July 20, 1988, I met an old acquaintance from my collegiate ministry. He shared openly about his past struggles with homosexuality and emotional dependency and the healing process that God had done in his life through a live-in program for ex-gays in California. I remember thinking, *I want that, too*.

Within a few weeks I applied to the same live-in program. However, by the fall of that year, I was out of fellowship—making every wrong choice possible based on a horrible 'last-fling' mentality. My last six weeks before moving to California turned into one long chain of sin. It seemed like Satan's last-ditch attempt to keep me in bondage. But I could smell freedom, so I sold all my belongings and flew to San Rafael.

I arrived on January 1, 1989. I was completely shut down emotionally, in great denial, rebellious and reeking of sin. But I'd come out to yield and heal, and this is where it began.

Jesus had been my Saviour for five years. I was well-grounded in his word and had ample knowledge about him—but he was still not Lord of my life. At our opening house retreat, a man with the gift of prophecy prayed over each one of us. I was very afraid and sceptical of charismatic activity, but when he spoke into my life, the words made a deep impression. 'You are like a wild black stallion,' he told me, 'strong and powerful, but needing to be gentled and tamed. God will change your fighting into submission, so that at his slightest whispered command, you will obey.'

This man knew my deepest desire for total obedience to the Lord. I was amazed—there was a lot more to God than I'd previously realised.

A month later I went to an all-church women's retreat up in the redwood forest. There my life was irrevocably changed. The conference title was, 'Come Away My Beloved', and its theme song, 'I Will Change Your Name', written by D J Butler.

> I will change your name, you shall no longer be called
> Wounded, outcast, lonely, or afraid.
> I will change your name, your new name shall be:
> Confidence, joyfulness, overcoming one,
> Faithfulness, friend of God, one who seeks my face.

© *1987 Mercy Publishing/Thankyou Music,*
Po Box 75, Eastbourne, BN23 6NW, UK.

So, on a drizzly, chilly Saturday in the stump of a burned-out redwood tree, I completely yielded my whole heart to

God. He became my Lord. I knew there was no turning back. He promised to change my name from Rebellious to Yielded, and end my truncated, abbreviated life to one of complete fullness. As my memorial to this event, I began to use my full name from that day on. Debbie became Deborah. I dropped all abreviations and nicknames, and my 'official signature' went from a scrawled set of impersonal initials to the fullness of my whole name. This was one indication of God replacing the cheap, surrogate, imitation things in my life with his truth and reality. From that point on, my life began to change significantly. Once I wilfully chose to submit, he had room to work in me.

God also gave me a key to unlock my emotions: singing. I love to sing, so he showed me that if I would sing out my hurts and feelings, they could come to the surface and be healed. Through the vehicle of song I brought up and experienced anger towards my parents for the very first time.

In the aftermath of this emotional storm, God's love broke through. Into my heart I received his love as never before. I had a wonderful sense of being a newborn baby, cradled in her daddy's arms: warm and secure, and looking up to see his eyes of love for the very first time. I remember later running across a field, delighting in my newfound discovery. 'My daddy loves me!' I hollered to myself over and over again. It was so much fun! The very next morning God confirmed that my hungry, desperate quest to be known was ended. He used a verse I had read countless times. 'Oh LORD, thou hast searched me and known me' (Ps 139:1, KJV). Like the velveteen rabbit, I felt I had become real. That began a major movement toward wholeness.

Throughout my life, my personhood was vague to me. I had no sense of self or boundaries. I didn't know where I stopped and someone else began. That left me with a compelling drive towards emotional dependency. If I was nobody, then I could change like a chameleon, reflecting whatever woman around me displayed the most dominant personality at the time. Then God showed me the truth since childhood: I had simply transferred my emotional dependency from person to person. These were not separate relationships—they were more like one single 'serial dependency'. Sometimes they even took on subtle, civilised forms, giving the illusion of 'normal' relationships, while actually just growing more ugly and strong.

Once I could see the whole picture, God asked me to renounce my emotionally dependent identity and release it. Letting go of that identity of being an idolatrous, emotionally dependent person was the scariest and hardest thing I've faced so far. It meant giving up what little identity I thought I had, no matter how wrong or false. It meant being laid bare before the Lord and trusting him to build a true identity in me, showing me the woman he created. It meant saying 'no' to myself and actively disciplining my dependent thought patterns.

Finally gaining a sense of freedom from that bondage was so awesome! It was really fun getting to know myself for the first time. Of course, this all happened gradually. While God prepared me to let go of the lies, he simultaneously built up my sense of self. He always laid down the foundation in advance before asking me to take the next step of healing.

Interestingly, as my life and identity have come into sharper focus, so has the healing process. What was vast and unknown two years ago has narrowed down to a need for boundaries and protection. And now I'm much more prepared to face them. My security in Christ has increased astronomically!

I believe next year will be the year that I begin to face the results of my earlier sexual abuse. Only recently I realised that my problems with trust, and especially trusting men, stemmed from the abuse. God's timing is perfect. Ever the gentleman, he never imposes or does things out of order. And in his sovereignty, he orchestrates our lives to help us face what we need to face. An unless we are confronted with issues, we tend to ignore them.

Meanwhile, I'm learning to build relationships with Christian men. Where God is leading for the distant future, I don't know. For now he is calling me to a new phase of my life. As I continue to submit and obey his loving guidance, my relationship with Jesus will grow sweeter and deeper. That is what healing is all about—the freedom to receive his love and then share it with others. By far the greatest reward of all is getting to know him, and becoming a reflection of Christ's love, redemption and restoration.

Marie's story

It seems like I have lived two lives. In a sense, I have. Six years ago, I was living as a lesbian with no thought or prospect of changing my lifestyle. Now I am married; I share my home, bed, life and heart with a man.

Some lesbian women marry to 'escape or flee' from their lifestyle, or think that by marrying, their feelings for a man will change. They believe marriage will 'fix' their problems with homosexuality. This is not my life or story. A shift and re-orientation has taken place in my heart and life, though it did not happen overnight and it definitely was not easy. I didn't marry to flee from lesbianism. I married because I fell deeply in love with a man.

It seems that most little girls dream about their wedding day and life with their Prince Charming. Not me. While other girls looked through bridal magazines and planned the colour scheme of their wedding and what their wedding dress would look like, I was busy playing basketball and every other sport under the sun. I had little interest or vision of marriage and life with a man.

Two major ongoing experiences occurred during my childhood and influenced this lack of vision. The first was incest. An older cousin abused me sexually when I was seven years old, and repeated this violation periodically over the next eight years. The second experience was being told, by my elder sibling, of my father's unfaithfulness to my mother. This knowledge devastated me. I remember coming to a conclusion. *If my own father could not be faithful to my mother, a man could not be faithful to me.* An inner vow took root. *I will never trust myself to a man.* I came to see men as abusive, domineering and adulterers. This viewpoint did not encourage relationships with men, let alone thoughts of marriage.

So, what happened? How did I end up married? I'll have to back up a little to share the events that culminated in marriage.

While in college, I met William. Although I deeply mistrusted men in general, I sensed something different about him. We shared mutually and built a deep and consistent relationship with each other. Will was the only man I had ever dated on a consistent basis.

After college, we went our separate ways. William became an overseas missionary, but we still kept in touch through letters and tapes. However, at that time I wasn't really interested in marriage to Will or any other man. A close friendship became dependent and I suddenly found myself in the arms of a woman. Being a lesbian certainly wasn't what I planned to be when I grew up. Still, it was a reality.

I had become a Christian at age thirteen. In the beginning of my lesbian involvement, I really turned my back on God. I didn't want Jesus to interrupt my life. But as time went on, my lesbian relationship started falling apart under the weight of our own neediness. We were draining each other of our very life-blood. As this was happening I started calling out to the Lord, wanting his presence. In the

midst of my pain, bondage and hopelessness, he intervened. God heard me and began filling me with a hope for
peace in my heart and a desire for change in my lifestyle.
Five months later, I moved out of our apartment and away
from my lover.

That period reminds me of David's prayer in Psalm 40. I
was poor in spirit and needy, and the Lord had mercy on
me and took me out of a pit of destruction. From this place
of calling out to the Lord for help, I contacted the local
Exodus referral ex-gay ministry. Immediately I started
being counselled and attending Living Waters, their
weekly group study programme.

It amuses and stuns me now to remember how small
my hopes were back then! All I wanted was peace of mind.
As I went through individual and group counselling, my
desire grew simply to be a secure, whole, celibate woman.
Thinking back now, I laugh to myself because I still did
not consider marriage as a possible option for me. I
remember telling the Lord that I would be happy to sleep
alone for the rest of my life.

My friend William and I had kept in touch over these
years. A deeper relationship was forming between us, so I
felt it necessary to tell him of my past lesbian involvement
and my desire to change. I thought he would turn away.
Actually, I sort of hoped he would so I wouldn't have to
deal with him any longer. Yet I also feared that I'd lose his
friendship.

I sent him a 'tell-all' tape. Will responded by saying that
my previous lesbian involvement didn't surprise him,
given my background. He reassured me that he still cared
for me, and he didn't drop our friendship! When he
returned to the States, he stayed close to me and supported
me emotionally. Relieved that Will was still in my life, I
was able to relax with him. I felt we both understood there
was no possibility for a romantic relationship.

Despite my determined effort to remain single and celibate, our friendship continued to deepen over the next few years. Meanwhile, I had to start dealing with many issues, including: trust, my viewpoint of men, emotional intimacy, fear of pain and loss, and personal insecurity and immaturity.

I felt that Will would eventually live up to my expectations of all men: hurtful, insensitive, unreliable, abusive and domineering. Because of my fears, I agonised over trusting him. I had difficulty sharing myself with him and asking him to do things for me. Although I doubted Will, he almost always surprised me by doing exactly what he told me he'd do. Will showed himself to be a man of integrity.

Yet, I still didn't fully trust him. I thought he would eventually change for the worse. Then I'd be hurt, disappointed and ultimately abandoned. I didn't want to be hurt again! Because of past pain, I wanted to play it safe. So I tried to protect myself by not risking with William. I guarded my heart from him. This was particularly obvious in my fear of emotional intimacy and lack of commitment to him. I'm sure Will wasn't totally aware of how ambivalent and torn I was regarding the depth and seriousness of our relationship.

Then, when I started to realise we were entering into a romantic relationship, I really panicked. A deep, internal unrest and anxiousness gnawed at me and continued to build. I walked around in agony for days: *You have got to get rid of Will, Marie. Do it. Do it now.* My fear and uneasiness finally diminished when I phoned Will to say that we needed to end our relationship.

My declaration didn't ruffle Will at all. He merely related that we should get together and talk about how I was feeling. We agreed on a time, and I determined to be done with this man.

The fateful day arrived. Will came and took me on a picnic. Then we went to the movies. Throughout the day, he affirmed that he cared for me and that I was a very special and wonderful woman. He said how thankful he was for me and our relationship. In essence, he wooed me, secured me and truly calmed me with his loving presence. At the end of our long day together, Will said, 'Now, Marie, what's this about ending our relationship?'

I broke into tears and my true feelings poured out. 'I don't want to lose you! I don't want you to go away, Will, but I don't know what to do with you either.' In my deep fear of loss and pain, I had decided to send William away before he hurt me. Surprisingly, the very next time I saw Will he asked me to marry him.

When Will proposed, all my pent-up insecurity poured out. 'I can't be a wife, Will. How could I sustain an intimate male-female relationship?' I was panicking. 'The wedding night just wouldn't work. An intimate, marital, sexual relationship between me and a man could never work!'

'But Marie,' he responded, 'you *are* involved in an intimate emotional relationship with me already and it's really working. We have the rest of our lives to work out all the difficulties.' What Will said next really penetrated my heart. 'I know you love me, Marie. So why are you doing this?'

I knew the reason: I felt so inadequate. I doubted my healing and my ability to be married. After all, I had been a lesbian. Only through the Lord's assurance of his presence and strength in my life could I finally say, 'Yes, William, I'll marry you.'

Some amazing things happened during our engagement period. Will and I travelled to my father's home state to visit my family and resolve some issues from my past.

After a time of prayer, I went alone (by choice) to talk with the cousin who had sexually abused me. 'I needed to come back and see you because a lot of bad things happened between us—hurtful, damaging things.'

My cousin looked at me. 'I know,' he said blandly.

Unsure of his feelings, I continued. 'I need to confront you about them.' I paused. There was still no reaction. I breathed deeply. 'Because,' I stuttered, 'because I'm going on with my life. And I don't want the things of the past hanging over me,' I finally spurted out.

We looked at each other. He did not ask for forgiveness, and I did not announce that I forgave him. Nevertheless, the confrontation was freeing for me. The acknowledgement that damage really did happen validated my emotions. So many times growing up, I thought I was crazy. *Did he really do those awful things to me? Or am I just making them up?* Now I knew. My memories were legitimate. I wasn't insane.

This experience broke down barriers and empowered me to talk all the more freely with Will about the abuse. What a comfort and encouragement he became to me the rest of that trip! We went to every single place where I'd been abused at the farm: the barn, garage, bathroom and fields. Together we walked through them, talking about what happened in each spot. No longer did the farm have a bigger-than-life death-grip on me. From then on, I would have new memories of those old places—me walking hand in hand with my fiancé.

It would be wonderful to say that the other 'difficulties' stopped immediately. They didn't. In engagement and marriage, I dealt with issues of loss of identity, fear of marital unfaithfulness, fear of dissatisfaction and unhappiness, and fear of sex.

As Will and I merged into a one-flesh union, I felt in some way that I was losing my own identity and sense of self. People now would say, 'Hi, Will and Marie.' It constantly reminded me that I was not just me any more. In prayer, the Lord revealed that I wasn't losing my own identity but that I was gaining more identity from him.

It was also very difficult for me to trust that Will would

be faithful both sexually and emotionally. I'd been hurt so much by infidelity that the thought that he wouldn't be true absolutely paralysed me. This issue is very deep for me. It's been incredible to be united with a man who is completely faithful! Will is so sensitive concerning this issue that he is guarded in his display of attention or affection to any other woman beside me. His loyalty has been healing and freeing.

Engaging in a relationship with a man is very different from relating with a woman. One thing I dreaded about marriage was the thought that Will could not really satisfy me. I feared not being totally happy with him, simply because he was a man. I feared discovering that women met my emotional and sexual needs better and more fully than Will. I was afraid that in discovering this, I would ultimately leave Will and return to the gay lifestyle.

Another major fear I had was sex! Sex with a man terrified me. I was afraid of engaging sexually with Will, despite the strong love I had for him. Deep wounds from my sexual abuse plagued me. Once I told Will, 'I can't really believe you have the same male sex organs that have brought me so much heartache, shame and pain in the past.' I also feared that Will would not be satisfied with me sexually. Maybe he would reject my body and not find me attractive, acceptable or desirable.

As I write these words, it's hard to believe I had such fears, but I did! I think they were valid, given my life experiences; yet I can honestly say that life is full, complete, emotionally rich and fun with Will. Our relationship is so incredibly superior to the measly scraps of emotional support and attention I received in the gay lifestyle.

It's been difficult to remember past struggles in my relationship with him. It seems now that relating with Will and sharing our life together is as natural and necessary as breathing. My past lesbian involvement doesn't consume and dominate our lives. Instead, we focus on other things—we actually have hopes and dreams together.

One of the biggest changes that has occurred is my desire not to be held in the arms of another woman, but to have my arms hold a child! My heart gets excited and joyful to think about our having children together. I am beginning to feel confident and assured that just as I've been a good wife to Will, I will also be a good and loving mum to our children.

Presently, Will and I both work at full-time jobs, but are involved as volunteers in ex-gay ministry. We're small group leaders for our ministry's programme. We love working with men and women who also want to leave their gay lifestyle. It is our dream to someday work full time together in ex-gay ministry. We desire to teach, counsel and guide others into abundant life in the Lord.

The process of change and healing continues. I have struggled with occasional homosexual desires and flash-backs from both my incest and involvement in the gay lifestyle. Yet—and it is a *big* yet—those are not the per-vading issues and struggles in my life. The good of my relationship with Will far outweighs the passing desires and flashbacks. The Lord and Will are the major focus of my desire and love. Our pervading problems are the bank account and laundry!

It *is* possible for your sexual orientation to change. It is also possible for a former lesbian to marry and to be happily married. I am, praise the Lord. He is faithful. And he can work in your life, just as he has worked in mine.

Julie's story

I was conceived only three months after my parents' mar-riage. My birth frightened my dad. He was faced with the new, awesome responsibility of fatherhood. Though Dad was faithful to bring home the pay cheque, he left all other responsibilities of family life to Mum.

During the first three years of my life I was very sick and was hospitalised for surgery several times. This proved a major source of deep feeling of abandonment. I was later told that after one of the surgeries, I wouldn't look into my mother's face for six entire months, and continually asked her, 'Why did you leave me?'

Four days after my third birthday, my sister was born. Already having internalised a lot of abandonment, I interpreted my sister's arrival as replacement. Perhaps this feeling of being replaced by a baby is what motivated me to abruptly reject all my 'babies' (in the form of dolls) and replace them with guns. From that point on, I rejected traditionally feminine patterns of play and gravitated toward things which would make me feel like a boy. Growing up, I loved rough and tumble play: fighting, army games, anything outdoors.

My mother always worried about my health and was excessively over-protective. I resented her for constraining my fun, neurotically worrying, and holding me back from experiencing life. This added to my further rejecting the goodness of femininity, since I believed that these negative traits my mother exhibited were fundamental to all women.

The early teenage years were the worst years of my life. My body had matured well beyond the other kids in my class. I became a very busty little girl. My sudden thrust into abounding womanhood must have been very intimidating to the scrawny boys in my class who felt insecure about their lack of physical maturity. I instantly became known as the class whore, although I had never kissed anyone. Each day, large groups of boys humiliated and shamed me by making fun of my body, associating it with something dirty.

In the summertime I was repeatedly molested by groups

of boys who would gang up on me at the local swimming pool. I hated what was happening to me. Yet I kept going back to the pool, desperately hoping to somehow find acceptance from my peers.

Also during this time, I found myself engaging in long, romantic fantasy scenarios about my best friend, Cheryl. These feelings frightened me and led me to pray, 'Oh, God, don't let me be a homosexual!'

Throughout my teenage years, I continued to fall in love with my girlfriends. Yet I dated boys because that was socially acceptable. Though I could never connect with boys in a fulfilling way, something inside me wouldn't let me accept that I was a homosexual.

Once, a girlfriend I had repeatedly fantasised about made a pass at me. It was a dream come true, yet something inside wouldn't let me go through with it. Although my sexual desires were strong, they greatly conflicted with my value system.

I became a Christian at age seventeen. By then I was using drugs daily to numb the pain I felt in my soul. At my conversion, I was instantly free from my dependence on alcohol and drugs. My world changed radically! Jesus was so real to me!

A few months later I discovered that being a Christian didn't take away the one thing which bothered me the most: my lesbian yearnings. I soon found myself falling into dependent relationships with women in my church.

I began to pray desperately that God would take away my homosexual tendencies and make me 'normal' so that I wouldn't sin against him. Even though I had never actually fallen sexually, I felt a lot of shame because I believed that the yearnings were sinful in themselves.

About three years after my conversion, I joined a missionary society. I began to sublimate my sexual feelings through radical Christian service. Within another three years, I'd become a well-respected leader in the mission.

Underneath, I continued to suppress both my lesbian feelings and my need for healing. I used my strong will to stay out of sin in thought and deed.

After eight years of Christian service both at home and abroad, my will power began to wear thin. During an extremely stressful time, I fell into an emotionally intense relationship with a woman on my team. Although there was a lot of inappropriate touching and holding, things didn't go farther—by God's grace.

After being in this relationship for five emotionally-charged months, the woman who had become the centre of my world abruptly rejected me. The resulting pain and turmoil led me to break out of my religious pride and denial, and seek help.

I learned of a nearby Christian organisation dedicated to helping people gain healing from homosexuality, and I attended one of their conferences. I was overwhelmed by the grace and presence of the Lord which I felt in that place. The staff of this ministry seemed to be some of the most whole people I'd ever met. They didn't deal with their brokenness through religious activism (as was my custom), but rather, by receiving God's presence they were truly healed from the inside out.

Several months after the conference, I got into individual counselling at this ministry and attended their Living Waters programme. God began revealing to me the roots of my lesbian tendencies and emotional dependencies.

The first steps in my healing involved learning to experience my emotions and to receive from the Lord and others. Gradually I set aside the ways that I'd always used to survive: 'bucking up', suppressing my feelings and doing good works for God. The Lord began to heal my inability to feel emotions, and I started to identify the pain, anger and abandonment buried deep inside me. Learning to experience, name, and appropriately vent those feelings (both emotionally and physically) was truly freeing. Also,

I could tell 'anything' about myself to others in the ministry and not be shamed by them. This helped me become more at home with my feelings and, consequently, more integrated as a person.

And I had a lot to tell! After suppressing my homosexual yearnings for years, getting in touch with my emotions brought up a deluge of lesbian feelings, fantasies and attractions. This time I was determined not to suppress my lesbian feelings, as I had before. Instead, through the accountability and covering of skilled helpers, I resolved to work through these feelings without causing another person to stumble in the process.

Getting in touch with the grace of God was a new and awesome reality for me. Although I had known the Lord for over a decade, I had not understood his acceptance and grace towards me at a heart level. I had been legalistic and performance-oriented in my walk. Through receiving healing prayer and being under good teaching, I began to experience God's mercy and unconditional love, whether I was doing well or not. I also learned grace through the ex-gay ministry staff, who loved me 'warts' and all.

During this time, there was a lot of teaching going around about receiving healing from homosexuality through healthy, reparative, same-sex friendships. Though I still think that there is some truth in this idea, at that time I made finding the perfect group of friends an idol in my life, an idol which the Lord had to topple. I was vulnerable to this idolatry because deep inside me lay that unhealed, primal need for bonding with Mother.

Through a series of rejections over a three-year period, God taught me not to be emotionally bent in an unhealthy way toward women. At one point, my entire group of friends rejected me, due to a difficult decision which I helped to make as a point of conscience. For an entire winter, my usually fun-filled social life was reduced to weekends at home alone, crying before the Lord. These rejections accessed the deeper primal rejections which I felt at the core of my being. Slowly and painfully I learned that no woman (or man, for that matter) could meet those deepest of unmet needs. Often, I would sit before the Lord, feeling the pain and asking him to fill the emptiness. I gradually learned what it meant to have Jesus at the centre of my being and to practice the presence of God there. This was truly the work of the cross, though I hadn't yet understood it as such.

Another area which required attention in my healing process was the years of verbal and sexual abuse I had experienced from the boys in my neighbourhood. Subsequent to this was the way I felt about myself as a woman, with a body which was both feminine and sexual. My view of men also needed to change.

This healing occurred slowly for me over a period of several years. Frequently I got in touch with the anger deep within caused by those repeated violations of my being. Not wanting to suppress these feelings, as I'd always done before, I learned to vent the anger verbally to the Lord while I was alone in my room or car.

Each time I felt the emotions, worked them through, and then spoke forgiveness. Now I know that healing and forgiveness are like an onion with many layers. Often the same incidents may need to be addressed a layer at a time until we get to the core. It was also helpful to receive prayer from men and women at the ex-gay ministry.

Along my journey, the Lord began to heal me as a gender being. I became secure in my gender identity. Prior to this healing, I always felt androgynous inside, knowing that I surely wasn't a man, but not feeling comfortable as a woman either. Through the love and care of benevolent male authority figures and friends, and through the high value which my local ex-gay ministry put on women, I began to integrate the goodness of my femininity and experience some of those inner realities.

The greatest thing I'm currently learning is the work of the cross. For most of my Christian life I had seen the cross as only one-dimensional: the place where we receive forgiveness of sin. Now I'm learning that the cross of Jesus has many more aspects which are necessary to appropriate in order for the healing of the heart at its deepest levels. The cross of Jesus has the ability to lift up and out of me all the rejection, abandonment, loneliness, abuse and harsh words that I have ever experienced.

At a 'Pastoral Care Ministry' school taught by Leanne Payne, I learned an important prayer exercise which made this truth more real to me. Leanne told us to use the eyes of our heart to 'see' Jesus dying on the cross. She then told us to 'see' him drawing the specific sins or hurts up and out of us and drawing them into himself. Praise God that these foul things needn't be continuously recycled within us. They finally have a place to go and remain for ever!

I am learning to apply the deeper work of the cross to the places of my soul which still need it. As Jesus takes my specific sin and pain into himself, I ask his presence to fill the void. As the darkness exits my soul and his presence comes in, I am more raised up into who I really am—a feminine, heterosexual woman of God with much hope for the future.

I am very thankful for the Lord's work in my life, especially over the last five years. In accordance with Philippians 1:6, I know that there are yet many good changes to come.

Peggy's story

I was three months old when my dad left for World War II, and three and a half years old when he returned. At his homecoming, I stood at the top of the stairs—leaning over the railing as he entered the foyer below—and said, 'Hi, Daddy! Are you my daddy?' This story symbolises the emotional distance that would invade our relationship most of my life.

I remember hardly anything about my early years until I was about seven years old. One night, at bedtime, Dad came to say goodnight to my sister and me. After we said our prayers, he turned out the lights and left—or so I thought. A while later he let out a scary yell, which frightened me terribly. Then he laughed. Apparently this scenario happened often, for I distinctly remember fearing that Dad was always in the room at night.

Dad's work took him out of the house for days on end, and when he was home at weekends we would all be afraid of him. He gave us several reasons for being wary. First, he disciplined us heavily. He never hit us, but his verbal abuse sank deep into our souls. 'Don't you dare cry!' he used to threaten. So I learned to stuff all of my feelings way down inside. Whenever I hurt, a huge lump came up in my throat. That was so painful, but I would never cry again. Second, Dad drank a lot. He got ugly when he drank—slamming doors, verbally putting down my mum, and making fun of her in very sarcastic ways.

Our family didn't know how to communicate. We never talked about our feelings, news, politics, or things of interest. I could only talk with Mum, and we always tried to work out what was wrong with Dad. He was so 'shut down' emotionally. We blamed him for everything. Now, I often wonder what his life was like growing up.

Dad and I loved each other, despite his faults and my fears. A part of me admired him. He had a lot of good qualities—when he wasn't drinking! He was clean and neat, always on time, and a man of his word. But he was also a perfectionist, and that can be difficult for a child. I lived under the constant fear of doing something wrong. When Dad drank, he wasn't trustworthy. Consequently, I had a lot of mixed emotions going on inside me. *How is Dad going to act today?*

During the years before adolescence, I was a loner, except for one 'special girl friend', which led to sexual attraction and exploration.

The most devastating times for me came during my early teens. By then, I didn't like my parents. I didn't feel safe with or without them. I felt overwhelmed by feelings of insecurity. The neighbour couple became my parents' weekend 'drinking buddies'. Dad started having an affair with the wife which caused turmoil within our family. The whole family saw Dad cheating on my mum. I felt betrayed and confused. I had loved this neighbour woman a lot, but I came to hate her. I had loved my dad a lot, too, but also began to hate him.

My mum came to me for comfort, and Dad wanted me to drink with him. I felt dead inside, so I'd drink with him. Then Dad's sexual advances began. No actual intercourse ever took place, but we did just about every other kind of sexual act.

I was afraid of Dad, so wouldn't speak up against what he was doing. Meanwhile, I was angry at my mum. *Where is she? Why can't she work out what Dad is doing to me? Who can help me? What can I do?*

I felt so violated, both emotionally and physically, that I couldn't stand looking at Dad or even being in the same room with him. Finally, I rejected everything about him.

During adolescence, homosexual feelings really surfaced in me. I wasn't sure any longer about who I was or what would happen in my life. However, I was detached from Mum, hated my dad, and I wanted to hurt them both. So I felt justified in doing whatever I wanted— including the pursuit of a lesbian relationship. The first one lasted nine years. In that time, I drank heavily and also took 'recreational' drugs. I knew something was wrong, but my emotions were so buried that I couldn't 'feel' anything but emptiness.

Eventually I ended up in a psychiatric ward, diagnosed

as severely schizophrenic. During that period, I experienced a terrible break-up with my lover and got involved in a new relationship. A new start! A brighter future!

For a year-and-a-half we tried to make our relationship work, but failed. We were both headstrong. I was afraid and scared, miserable and dead inside. The void within me was so vast, so black, that nothing seemed to fill it.

I tried reading the Bible, but couldn't understand it. Then one day I heard a song about Jesus and my 'spiritual ears' were opened. A few weeks later I experienced the most frightening vision of black emptiness I'd ever known. But I also felt an overwhelming presence of peace and warmth which I now recognise as the Holy Spirit. I surrendered, and instantly knew my problem: I was separated from God. Somehow I knew that I needed Jesus to connect me with God, so I asked Jesus to enter my life and make me into the person he wanted. I began to experience the inner peace I'd been looking for all my life.

Ironically, my lover accepted Christ as Saviour approximately two weeks before I did. Neither one of us knew of the conversion of the other until we found each other reading the Bible. Changes started deep within both of us.

More than anything, I wanted to please God. As I grew, two things happened. First, the Lord began a divine division between my lover and me. Eventually, we stopped sleeping together. Second, the Holy Spirit swiftly convicted me of my need to honour my parents as Ephesians 6:2–3 commands. Also, I knew that unless I forgave my parents, especially Dad, I would be stuck forever in bitterness and hatred (see Mark 11:25).

I took his word seriously. I wanted it to be well with me. I wanted to experience peace in my parental relationships. I wanted to be free from the memories and ugliness and pain. But my pain ran so deep. Just thinking about my dad, I would almost throw up. Yet Jesus had forgiven and accepted me, so I knew I must also forgive Dad.

'God, please give me the desire to want to forgive Dad,' I begged. In the beginning, though, I didn't understand forgiveness. I thought that if I forgave Dad, I'd be re-opening all the emotional areas that he had violated—that I'd be exposing myself again to his hurting me. It helped greatly when I finally comprehended what forgiveness means. It doesn't mean that I agree with or deserve what some person did to me, or that what they did doesn't matter. No, forgiveness was simply choosing to release Dad from my vengeance. That enabled me to begin removing the hardness from my heart and clearing my communication with God. Perhaps now I could begin to experience release from my pain.

Then I pleaded with God, 'Give me a new heart for my father.' Even though I'd forgiven Dad, I wasn't yet experi-encing any freedom from the painful memories. I kept seeing 'pictures' in my mind of terrible events involving my father and me. God showed me that these 'instant replays' were a work of Satan to challenge the Lord's working in my life. I took authority over those awful memories and the lies of the devil. Every time they tried to haunt me, I commanded them to go in the name of Jesus. Also, I confessed out loud that I had forgiven my dad. It was a real battle, but victory eventually came.

Beside the whole issue of bad memories, the Lord gave me another clear choice. For years I had grumbled about my dad not meeting my needs. But I sensed God saying, 'You had much higher expectations than your father was ever able to fulfil, even if the verbal and sexual abuse had never taken place. Are you willing to accept the fact that your father will *never* be able to meet your needs?'

I was at a point of decision. One path was clinging to my 'rights' to hold hatred toward him. Or, I could let go of my dream of having a perfect father and allow God to bring healing.

I chose the latter, releasing all my expectations of the

'perfect' father. God would be my Father—I could trust that he would never hurt me. At that instant, I felt as though fifty tons had rolled off my back.

Time marched on. Then, in February 1982, my father was diagnosed with lung cancer. Chemotherapy started immediately. Mum could never get Dad to talk about the cancer, his feelings, or his fears. He just kept everything bottled up inside.

My greatest fear was that Dad would die without Christ. Interestingly, that fear showed me the depth of forgiveness I had actually experienced toward him. Why should I care about his eternal state if I still harboured any bitterness toward him? No, I really wanted Dad to know Jesus' love and forgiveness.

Due to Dad's illness, my sister came to know the Lord. (How thankful I am that my Mum now also knows Jesus.) But what about Dad? He didn't want to hear any of that 'religious talk' about God!

I asked my sister if she had told Dad about her new relationship with Christ. 'Do I really have to?' she asked. I encouraged her to speak with him.

The day after Christmas, Dad was very sick. My sister was talking with him on the couch when I heard her call me over.

'What is it?'

'Well,' she said, 'Dad doesn't understand that he needs to ask Jesus into his life in order to get to heaven.'

I kneeled down in front of my father and looked him straight in the eyes—something I had *never* been able to do. 'Pop, what is it you don't understand?'

'I don't believe in hell,' he said.

'It doesn't matter whether you believe in hell or not,' I answered. 'The Bible says that there is a hell, so there is a hell.'

'I want to be cremated,' he retorted.

I thought for a moment before answering. 'I don't

know what the Bible says about that, but one thing is for sure. Cremation will not be the end of you. Your spirit will leave your body when you die, and you'll be eternally separated from God.'

Leaning forward, I continued. 'Pop, we're a family. We're going to heaven and we want you with us!'

His face relaxed, and then he said the words I'd prayed for years to hear: 'What do I have to do?'

During the next few minutes, my sister and I had the glorious honour of leading our dad to the Lord. He prayed with us and asked for God's forgiveness and accepted Christ as his Saviour.

I didn't see the kind of changes in him that often accompany conversion. He was too ill to read the Bible or tell others about Jesus. But I did see God working within him. My dad had been a very bitter, caustic, angry man. All that seemed to fall away as the Lord's Spirit gave him a new calm and peace. I sensed that he felt God's love.

Another important event took place before Dad died the following June. He'd never spoken to me about my former lesbian involvement, but I knew he was ashamed of me. The cancer had gone to his brain by then and I wasn't really sure he would understand what I was about to say, but it was so heavy on my heart that I just had to tell him.

I leaned over him and talked quietly. 'Pop, I never really was the daughter you expected me to be. I'm so sorry about that. Please forgive me.'

Dad gave no visible response, but I continued on anyway. 'You know, you weren't the father I expected either. But I've forgiven you. And God's given me such a love for you, Pop.'

The whole time I talked, Dad said nothing to me at all. Whether he comprehended me then or not, I have such joy in knowing that from his heavenly vantage-point now he sees all the work God has done and is doing in my life. And I know Dad must be very pleased.

It has been eight years since Dad died, and my growth goes on. God has done such a marvellous work in my life and my heart. As he released me from hatred, unforgiveness and bitterness, my bondage to homosexuality was broken. And he has given me true love and forgiveness toward my precious parents. How I thank him, for now I love them the way he always intended.

If it can happen for me—the victim of terribly broken relationships with my parents—there's hope for you.

CHAPTER FOURTEEN

CHOOSE YOUR MOUNTAIN

The life we live is largely dependent on the choices we make. We are not autonomous in our decision making, but are strongly influenced by people around us and by what we hear and read. Unfortunately, many people are more likely to place their trust in man's interpretation of a situation, rather than to trust in God. An example of this misplaced trust can be found in the book of Numbers.

The Hebrews were near the promised land when God directed Moses to send out twelve spies. Their mission was one of reconnaissance.

> 'See what the land is like and whether the people who live there are strong or weak, few or many. What kind of land do they live in? Is it good or bad? What kind of towns do they live in? Are they unwalled or fortified? How is the soil? Is it fertile or poor? Are there trees on it or not? Do your best to bring back some of the fruit of the land' (Num 13:18–20).

Clearly, Moses had no idea what to expect from this promised land. The questions he had are not dissimilar to those a woman asks about heterosexuality: *What do straight women talk about? Do 'healthy' women hug? If so, for how long a time? What do they do for hobbies?*

The spies spent forty days exploring the land God had given them. They returned to the camp laden down with grapes, figs and pomegranates. The land was obviously very fertile. Although ten of the spies did not deny the obvious richness of the land, fear of man outweighed all the blessings that Canaan could offer. Their focus was not on the goodness of the land, but on the difficulties they would encounter. They summed up the situation as follows:

> 'The land we explored devours those living in it. All the people we saw there are of great size... We seemed like grasshoppers in our own eyes, and we looked the same to them' (Num 13:32–33).

Even though the land was promised to them, the spies trusted their own emotions rather than God. Their bad report incited the rest of the Israelites to turn against him.

> That night all the people of the community raised their voices and wept aloud. All the Israelites grumbled against Moses and Aaron, and the whole assembly said to them, 'If only we had died in Egypt! Or in this desert! Why is the Lord bringing us to this land only to let us fall by the sword? Wouldn't it be better for us to go back to Egypt?' And they said to each other, 'We should choose a leader and go back to Egypt' (Num 14:1–4).

The Hebrews refused to take God at his word. Fear and unbelief encouraged them to look at their past life. Once again, Egypt looked inviting. The certainty of slavery was more appealing than a mere promise of something better. God cannot tolerate unbelief, and, over a period of forty years, he allowed a whole generation of people to die. Their sin prevented them from entering Canaan. Only

Caleb and Joshua, the two spies who chose to believe God, walked into the promised land.

What are your chances of success?

There are many women who have 'tried to go straight' and have failed. Perhaps their vision for change died, or they were influenced by the world, or felt overwhelmed by seemingly insurmountable difficulties. Whatever the reason, they, like the ten spies, found the task too daunting. We must not be surprised or discouraged when we hear of failure. Jesus teaches that the gate to eternal life is narrow (Mt 7:13–14). Similarly, the gate to wholeness in Christ is also narrow, and not everyone will walk that path.

Twelve leaders were chosen to scout out the land of Canaan. Ten of those leaders failed to see beyond the difficulties to the blessings that lay ahead for those who trust in God. They chose to remain where they were in the desert rather than seize hold of the opportunity for a new life. These ten leaders did not know their God.

The parable of the sower in Matthew chapter 13 describes four different kinds of people who hear the gospel. According to this parable, only twenty-five per cent of people follow Jesus wholeheartedly! Seventy-five per cent of people either ignore the word, have a brief walk with Jesus, or become so ensnared by the world that their walk into wholeness is ruined.

Where do you stand today? Are you walking on a narrow path? Are you one of the two spies who has a good report of the land? Are you one of the twenty-five per cent of Christians who will run their race with perseverance?

Be a Caleb

Caleb was not a dreamer. He knew that to enter the promised land would be hard. There would be battles to fight and people to overthrow. But Caleb knew his God.

> 'Only do not rebel against the LORD. And do not be afraid of the people of the land, because we will swallow them up. *Their protection is gone, but the LORD is with us.* Do not be afraid of them' (Num 14:9, italics mine).

Caleb's cry was not popular and there was a call to stone him. But God always recognises and rewards a true believer.

> 'No one who has treated me with contempt will ever see it. But because my servant Caleb has a different spirit and follows me wholeheartedly, I will bring him to the land he went to, and his descendants will inherit it' (Num 14:23–24).

Caleb's belief in God did not fizzle out over time. Even though it took a further forty-five years before Caleb saw the promised land again, his enthusiasm for God did not wain in that time.

> 'So here I am today, eighty-five years old! I am still as strong today as the day Moses sent me out; I'm just as vigorous to go out to battle now as I was then. Now give me this hill country that the Lord promised me that day. You yourself heard then that the Anakites were there and their cities were large and fortified, but, *the LORD helping me, I will drive them out just as he said*' (Josh 14:10–12, italics mine).

Caleb had long-term vision. He needed that to sustain his enthusiasm for the workings of God. Caleb had tasted of the promised land and he knew that it was not a figment of the imagination. How tempting it must have been for Caleb to have questioned God. Forty-five years is a long time to retain hope, especially when those around you seek to drag you down into their despair. But Caleb was not content to merely enter the promised land—he chose the hardest area to conquer, a mountain, the stronghold of the Anakites. He trusted God to fulfil his promise about the land. Caleb was not content to wander about in the safety of the foothills; he wanted complete possession of the land.

As ex-lesbians, we need to be Calebs. We need hope, a long-term vision and complete trust in God. Understanding that the change process is not an overnight phenomenon helps offset frustration. Just as we did not suddenly become lesbians, we will not suddenly become heterosexual. There is no 'quick fix' method to healing.

But healing is a reality.

The choice is yours. You can choose to remain in Egypt, in the bondage of lesbianism. You can choose to compromise your Christian walk and leave Egypt, but remain close to the border. You can choose to wander in the desert for years because of unbelief and complaining. Or you can walk through the desert and into the promised land of wholeness in Christ.

> Forget the former things; do not dwell on the past. See, I am doing a new thing! Now it springs up; do you not perceive it? I am making a way in the desert and streams in the wasteland... to give drink to my people, my chosen, the [women] I formed for myself that they may proclaim my praise (Is 43:18–19,21).

God is doing a new and wonderful thing in many women's lives. He can do the same for you. Change is possible. You do not have to be trapped in the bondage of lesbianism. You do not have to walk aimlessly in the desert. God has a plan for you, a plan that will prosper you. Catch the vision for change, and join us in our walk into the promised land!

APPENDIX
GUIDELINES WHEN LOOKING FOR HELP

God does provide many resources for us as we seek to overcome our lesbian background. The major ones are:

1. Our own regular study of the Bible, our own prayer times, and our own leaning on the Holy Spirit for guidance in what to do. Our relationship with the Lord is of primary importance to our growth and healing.
2. A local church body, with its various ministries: worship and teaching, Bible study groups, special ministries for women and single people.
3. An accountability relationship, which we can often develop within the context of a church small group Bible study or a support group.
4. Private counselling and/or ex-gay ministries.

General approach

The following guidelines are geared to those women who are seeking to find a church. However, the questions can easily be adapted to cover other situations, including counselling services and Christian ministries.

It is less stressful to phone churches or ministries before visiting. In this way you can ask very pertinent questions without fear of embarrassment for either party.

Absolute essentials

The following questions deal with fundamentals of the Christian faith. If a church, support group, or counselling ministry cannot answer 'yes' to all of these questions, they do not really believe the Bible. Avoid such groups. Do not bother asking them any other questions about their ministry or activities.

- Do you believe the Bible is the inspired, inerrant Word of God?
- Do you believe in the Trinity?
- Do you believe in the deity, humanity, virgin birth, and sinless life of Christ?
- Do you believe that Jesus' death on the cross paid for all our sins, and that believing on Him is the only way to heaven?
- Do you believe Jesus is coming back?
- Do you believe in heaven and hell?

Worship style and minor points of theology

If a church agrees with all the fundamental doctrines of Christianity, you may want to ask them about their worship style. Some women prefer a more solemn style of worship, with traditional hymns and a quiet, meditative mood. Others prefer a more active style, with praise songs and raising of hands in worship.

Inquire about other aspects of the church's theology that matter to you personally, such as whether they are charismatic or non-charismatic.

These are up to your own discretion. However, do not

totally write off a church because of differences of opinion involving worship style or what you consider to be relatively minor doctrinal issues. God works through many different groups.

Investigating attitudes

Assuming a church has the correct basic theological framework, what next? Explore their views on spiritual growth and overcoming life-dominating sin problems. Ask open-ended questions which will expose their attitudes and definitions of the process of healing.

- How does spiritual growth take place?
- Do you believe there is any life-dominating sin outside God's ability or desire to heal?
- How would you handle this situation: A single woman who was sexually abused as a child comes into your congregation. What would you do to help her?
- How would you help someone struggling with an overwhelming sin problem like alcoholism or sexual addiction? What would you do if they were okay for a while, but then fell back into sin?
- Do you believe homosexuality is sin? (I would suggest this not be your very first question.)

You want to know if they will encourage you personally and spiritually in your journey. So beware if they give you defeatist answers, like 'Just stop it', or generalities like, 'Pray and God will take care of it.'

After hearing their answers to some of these questions, you may feel comfortable enough to disclose your own struggles and ask what they could offer in your situation.

Ministry opportunities

The following questions are for churches which have passed the 'doctrine test'.

- Do you believe in intimate, small groups as a context for Christian growth? What kind of groups or Bible studies do you offer? What goes on at a typical group meeting? Is there open, vulnerable sharing so that people can get to know each other better? Do your groups exercise accountability? Do your groups just study the Bible, or do they pray for one another in important areas of each other's life?
- How do you feel about accountability? How does your church define accountability?
- Do you have a women's ministry or women's discipleship programme? If so, what do they do?
- Do you have a ministry for single people? What is it like?
- Do you have any kind of special support groups for people who want to overcome life-dominating sin problems or other issues, like sexual abuse (or homosexuality)? Are they up to hearing the truth of what is happening in my life?
- Do you offer counselling in your ministry?

Do not limit your choices only to those churches with support groups or ex-gay ministries. There are many churches with caring people and loving pastors who have never before had someone in church who was leaving a homosexual lifestyle. Yet these churches can be very supportive and be intimately involved in helping each other grow.

It is important for you to go to the women's meetings and single events, even if you do not feel you fit in. But do not expect the church to be everything you need. Only God can do that.

No church is immediately home to anyone. Give it some time. Attend for at least a month before you decide to stay or leave, unless it is clearly not in accordance with Christian fundamentals. You will never find a perfect church. If later on you sense new needs, pray about the possibility of changing churches. However, do not play 'revolving churches' just to avoid your responsibilities or to avoid being confronted with truth from God's word.

GLOSSARY OF TERMS

Abundant life

Living life to the full, according to standards God lays out in the Bible. An abundant life is full of enjoying God, accepting self, spiritual growth and service to others. Not everything is pleasant in such a life, but the Christian finds meaning in suffering as God uses those difficult circumstances to his glory and the Christian's growth.

Abandonment

To leave someone alone physically or emotionally. Leave feeling empty, lonely or isolated.

Accountability/
Accountable

Placing yourself under the authority of a Christian, usually one who is more mature than you. Often you share the most sensitive or hurting aspects of your life with this person. You also give this 'overseer' permission to ask you directly how you are doing in general, and specifically

267

in areas of temptation. The accountable person commits to share her thoughts, struggles and feelings, plus openly confess her sins. Success in an accountability relationship depends on: (1) God and his word being at the centre; (2) a balance of compassion and firmness by the 'overseer'; and (3) a desire to change/grow, and vulnerability on the part of the accountable person.

Act out — To carry out in a physical, overt way your internal fantasies, emotions and wishes.

Affirm — Spoken approval and acceptance, usually accompanied by direct eye contact, and often with physical touch. Affirm and disapprove are opposites.

Androgyny — Feeling and acting like a 'third sex', neither male nor female, but some nebulous combination in between the two.

Blame shifting — Instead of accepting your own responsibility and consequences in a problem situation, you try to make things look like someone else is responsible for the problem. (Adam and Eve in the garden.)

Boundaries — Where a person and their responsibilities begin and end. Lack of boundaries means not being able to distinguish between oneself and others.

Broken femininity	Operating in an unbalanced way, often stressing one's masculine attributes to the detriment of the feminine.
Christian walk/ life	A term describing the overall behaviour of a person in line with God's commands. All that we should think, say and do.
Commitment	A determination to be and/or do certain things, followed up with appropriate actions to accomplish those goals.
Conditional love	Love with strings attached. You have to do something in order to get something. Reward/punishment system. ('I will love you if you get high marks in school.')
Control	Making people and circumstances revolve around one's self, whether through 'negative', overt means (such as verbal abuse) or 'positive' means (such as flattery). Two ends of the control-issues spectrum are: (1) the strong, overpowering, dictating type of woman; and (2) the weak, 'doormat', subservient type of woman. As a friend of mine says, 'Manipulators and martyrs go together in sets.'
Death to self	Denying one's own impulses to act or react in a particular manner in favour of operating under God's guidelines.

Defence system/ Defence mechanism	Any means we use to deflect other's attempts to get close to us emotionally or to criticise us. Or it may be any attempts on our part to deny personal responsibility in a matter.
Denial	Failure or refusal to acknowledge the reality that a problem exists. Lying to oneself about a problem, and one's own responsibility in it. Cope by disavowing an event or refusing to face it.
Distance (verb)	The opposite of vulnerable. Closed off emotionally.
Emotional absence	A person may be physically present, but may not involve themselves emotionally in the life of another.
Emotional dependency	The condition resulting when the ongoing presence and/or nurturing of another is believed necessary for personal security. (From the booklet, *Emotional Dependency: A Threat to Close Friendships*, by Lori Thorkelson Rentzel, pp 1–2.)
Enmesh	In this instance, enmeshment means an intertwining of two people's emotions, decision-making, and subsequent actions. It is an unhealthy intertwining of two people which violates personal boundaries and individual lives.

Fall, falling, fell	In a Christian context, these terms refer to entering into sin. Ultimately, a person chooses to fall into sin, regardless of whether succumbing to a temptation feels otherwise. (For example, you might make excuses for your choice: 'I couldn't avoid it. I've gone this far — might as well go all the way.')
Femininity	Attributes and characteristics of being a woman, which is a balance of the masculine and the feminine. The essence of what God intends women to think, feel and act like. A truly feminine woman honours God in all these aspects of her life. Femininity has a different balance of attributes than does masculinity. Femininity is more soft, yielded, responsive, nurturing and receptive. Masculinity relates more to authority, decisiveness and assertiveness. Women should have both sets of qualities, but more emphasis on the feminine ones.
Flesh	The sinful, broken nature found in all human beings. The flesh always pulls us toward self-centredness, self-protection and self-gratification.
Gay lifestyle	No one particular way of living constitutes a 'gay lifestyle', but it is general activity centred on one's sexual orientation.
Gender	The physical sex I was born with, by God's design.

Gender identity

The sex I affiliate myself with. Although a woman may cognitively accept that she is female, she may not emotionally identify with that status. Confusion occurs when a woman does not feel 'right' in the body or status she sees.

God-centred life

An individual's life revolves around who God says she is, and his expectations of her. God is central to all of her thoughts and subsequent actions. Her aim is to follow him and not her own whims.

Growth/Healing process

The process of change to be more like Christ, which is the goal God intends for us. Growth involves our learning about God from the Bible; choosing to accept and act upon truth; responding to the Holy Spirit; being honest with God, ourselves, and others about our victories and failings; and relating vulnerably with other Christians.

Guilt (two senses)

(1) I have done wrong, deserve punishment, and experience suitable emotional reaction to predicament.

(2) I have set too high a standard for myself, and berate self for inability to meet unreal expectations. Emotional response occurs due to a mixture of anger, frustration and sense of inadequacy.

Heart knowledge

Accepting something spiritually and emotionally as well as on an intellectual level.

Inner vow

A commitment, usually unspoken, involving 'always' or 'never', to do certain things or be a certain way.

Intimacy

The term *intimacy* is often used of sexual contact, but that is not its primary meaning. True intimacy is the sense of personal, emotional closeness between two people in a relationship. In an intimate relationship, both partners are vulnerable (willing to share their innermost thoughts, feelings and hurts) and focused on meeting the various needs of the other partner.

Lesbian lifestyle(s)

Variety of activities and attitudes within those women functioning in some type of lesbianism.

Lesbianism

Three categories, all trying to find completion of self, a sense of wholeness, within real or imagined relationships with other women. First, women who strive to fulfil sexual desires and emotional needs through other women. Second, women who have not acted out sexually, but sought completion through an emotional relationship with another woman. Third, those women who are too frightened to act upon their desires, so they resort to fantasy.

Lust

Strong desire for something God says will hurt us and our relationships. Ultimately, lust is an illegitimate longing for something contrary to God's character and will for us.

Manipulate	Gaining control over a person or situation using underhand or devious means. It is a covert form of control.
Mindset	Establishing a certain way of thinking, and operating under those restraints.
Minimisation	You acknowledge having a certain problem, but act as though it isn't really very significant to one's present-day living.
Misbelief	Any thought we cling to that is contrary to what God says is true. We often hold on to misbeliefs about who God is, who we are, who other people are, how we should relate to other people, etc. We can counteract misbeliefs with the truth and acting on the truth.
Mother issues	A general term pertinent to matters concerning the attitudes a daughter fosters with regard to her mother.
Nurture	To nourish and care for someone or something.
'Real' needs	Often we, wittingly or unwittingly, confuse our needs with our desires. Often our true needs never surface because we are too keen to minister to our desires. By denying ourselves the opportunity to satisfy our desires, we allow God to unveil our true needs.
Release in my spirit/the Spirit	A feeling of relief or peace after feeling burdened, concerned or fearful.

Relinquish	Give up something; turn it over to someone else.
Renounce	To consciously acknowledge a sinful attitude or behaviour, and determine not to become involved with that problem again.
Repent/ Repentance	Turn from our sins and reliance on self, and turn toward God and reliance on his word and Spirit.
Repression	Forgetting, hiding or submerging a memory that is emotionally painful. The problem continues to affect current actions, however.
Self-protection	Using a variety of defence mechanisms to avert any ensuing intimacy with God or others. Actions to prevent further hurt.
Spiritual brokenness	A condition of having problems and struggles, whether you realise it or not.
Spiritual realm	According to Ephesians 6, the unseen realm of God, angels and human spirits, where battles are waged over us and our souls.
Third sex	A middle ground based on one's confusion over fact ('I am a woman') and feeling ('I don't feel like a woman').
Trauma	The list is endless, but it does include emotional abuse, verbal abuse, death in the family, separation, divorce, hospitalisation.

Unconditional love	Love shown to you all the time, in spite of the fact that often you don't really deserve it because of your failings and flaws.
Victimisation	Events, attitudes and actions that happen to you over which you have little or no control. For instance, being born into a family where one parent is an alcoholic.
Vulnerable/ Vulnerability (two senses)	(1) To be susceptible to attack.

(2) To open yourself to others emotionally for the purpose of establishing a relationship. |

INFORMATION

The following organisations have information on those ex-gay ministries currently affiliated to Exodus International. They will direct you to the nearest ministry in your area. All telephone numbers require the relevant international dialling code if phoning from outside that country.

North America

Exodus International–North America
PO Box 77652
Seattle, WA 98177
USA
Telephone: 206-784-7799
Toll Free in USA: 1-888-264-0877
Fax: 206-784-7872
Internet: www.exodusintl.org

Europe/Africa

Exodus International–Europe
PO Box 407
Watford
UK
Telephone: 44-181-420-1066
Fax: 44-181-421-1692
E-mail: exodus.europe@btinternet.com
Internet: www.exoduseurope.org

Latin America/Brazil

Exodus Internacional Latinoamerica
Centro aereo 1Q1534
Miami, FL 33152-1534
E-mail: Exodusla@juno.com

South Pacific–Asia

Exodus South Pacific
Suite 256
45 Cribb St.
Milton, Queensland 4064
Australia
Phone/Fax: 07-3371-4705
E-mail: Exodus@in4free.com.au

Exodus International

International Exodus Headquarters
PO Box 21039
Ajax Ontario
Canada L1H 7H2
Telephone: 905-686-7363
Fax: 905-686-1716

Regeneration Books

Regeneration
PO Box 9830
Baltimore
Maryland 21284
USA
Telephone: 410-661-4337
Fax: 410-882-6312
E-mail: Regenbooks@juno.com
Website: Linked from www.exodusintl.org

NOTES

1. Leanne Payne, *The Broken Image: Restoring Personal Wholeness Through Healing Prayer* (Crossway Books: USA, 1981), p 146 (UK edition: Kingsway Publications, 1988).
2. H Norman Wright, *Always Daddy's Girl* (Regal Books: USA, 1990), p 143.
3. Gerard van den Aardweg, *Homosexuality and Hope* (Servant Books: USA, 1985), p 72.
4. Wright, *op cit*, p 214.
5. Adapted from Lori Thorkelson Rentzel, *Emotional Dependency: A Threat to Close Relationships* (Exodus International: USA, 1987), pp 3–4.
6. J Oswald Sanders, *Enjoying Intimacy With God* (Moody Press: USA, 1980).
7. Elisabeth Elliot, *Loneliness* (Oliver-Nelson: USA, 1988), p 26 (UK edition: Kingsway Publications, 1990).
8. Floyd McClung, *The Father Heart of God* (Kingsway Publications: UK, 1985) (US edition: Harvest House, 1985), p 40.
9. Oscar Thompson, *Concentric Circles of Concern* (Broadman Press: USA, 1981).

10. Payne, *op cit*, pp 46–47.
11. Gary Inrig, *Quality Friendship: The Risks and Rewards* (Moody Press: USA, 1981), p 23 (adapted—I have changed the pronouns from masculine to feminine for easier application to our situation).
12. C S Lewis, *The Four Loves* (Harcourt Brace Jovanovich: USA, 1960), p 98 (UK edition: Fontana, 1963).
13. Leanne Payne, *Crisis in Masculinity* (Crossway Books: USA, 1985) (UK edition: Kingsway Publications, 1988).
14. Larry Crabb, *Inside Out* (NavPress: USA, 1988), pp 211–212.
15. Payne, *The Broken Image*, p 116.
16. Lois Mowday, *Daughters Without Dads* (Oliver-Nelson: USA, 1990), p 89.